Ghost Towns

and

Discontinued Post Offices

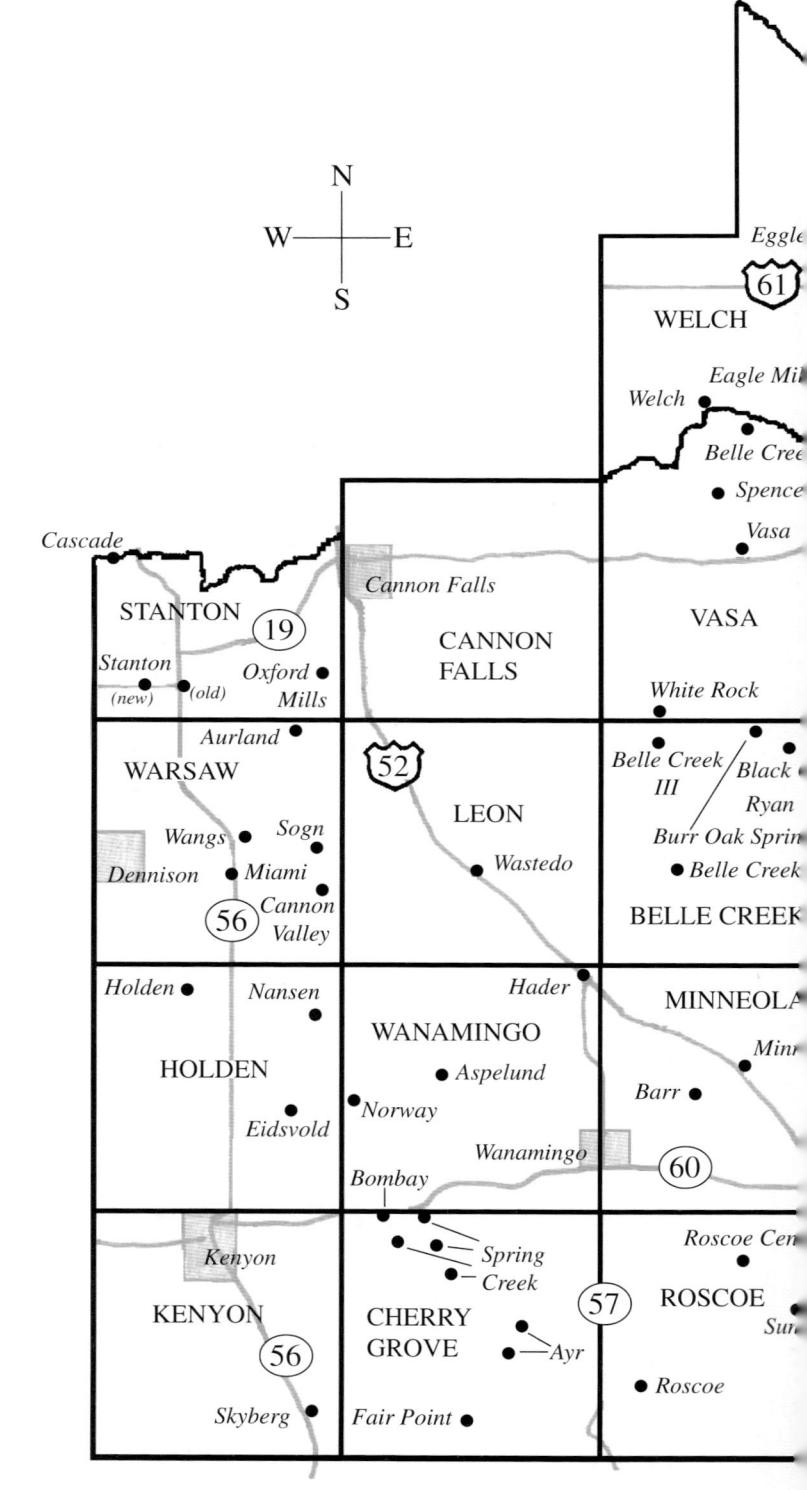

N
W — E
S

Eggle

61
WELCH

Eagle Mil

Welch ●
Belle Cree
● Spence

Vasa

Cascade ●

STANTON
19

Cannon Falls

CANNON
FALLS

VASA

Stanton
(new)
● (old)
Oxford ●
Mills

White Rock
●

Aurland ●

WARSAW

52

LEON

Belle Creek
III
● Black
Ryan
Burr Oak Sprin

Sogn
Wangs ●
●
● Miami
Dennison ●
56
Cannon
Valley

Wastedo ●

● Belle Creek

BELLE CREEK

Holden ●
Nansen
●

HOLDEN

Eidsvold ●

Hader ●

WANAMINGO

● Aspelund

● Norway

MINNEOLA

Minn
●

Barr ●

Wanamingo

60

Bombay

Kenyon

KENYON
56

Spring
Creek
● Creek
●

CHERRY
GROVE

57

Roscoe Cen
●

ROSCOE

Sur

● Ayr

● Roscoe

Skyberg ●

Fair Point ●

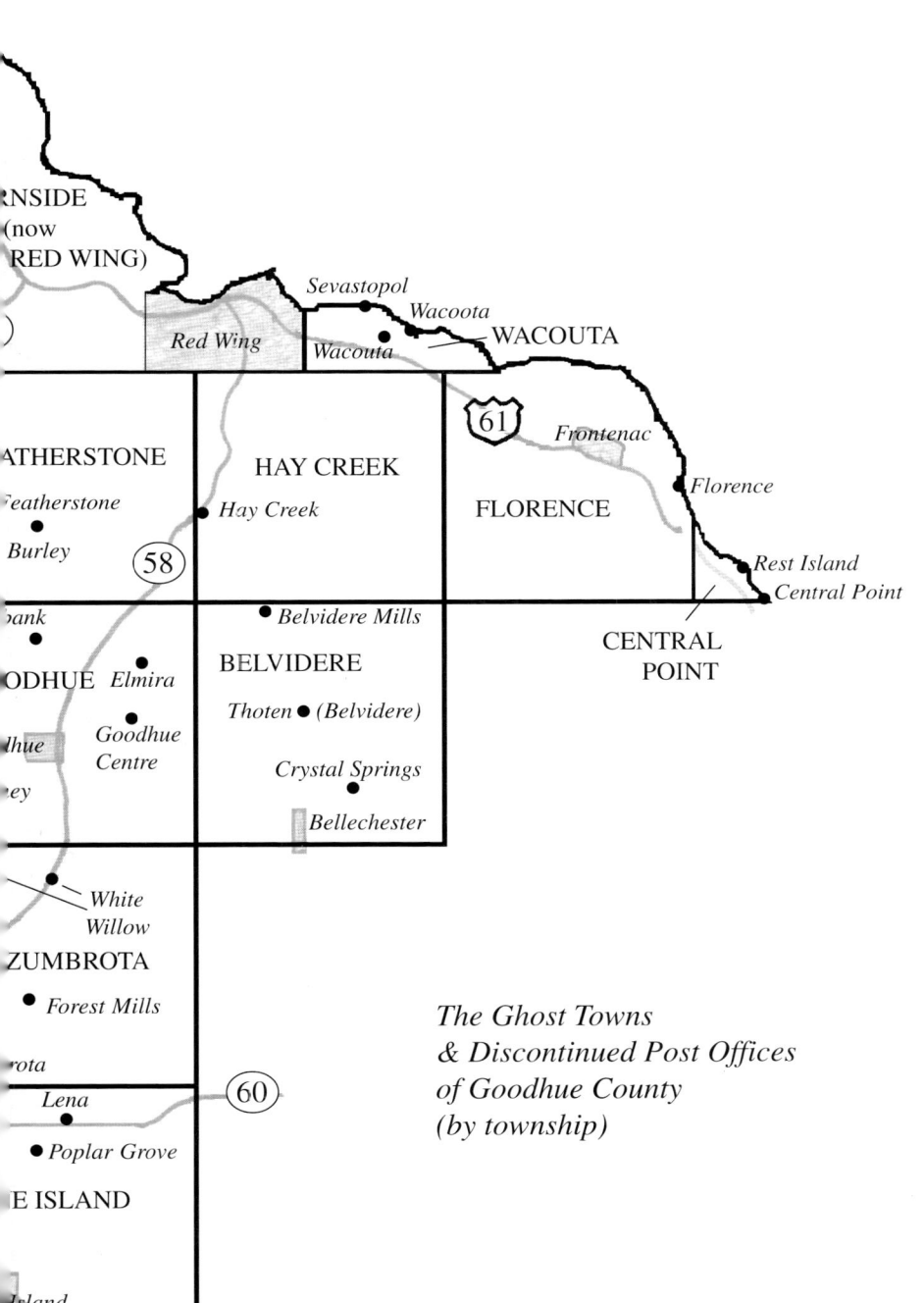

NSIDE
(now
RED WING)

)

Sevastopol

Wacoota

Wacouta ——— WACOUTA

Wacouta

Red Wing

61

Frontenac

ATHERSTONE

HAY CREEK

FLORENCE

Florence

Featherstone

Hay Creek

Rest Island

Burley

58

Central Point

bank

CENTRAL
POINT

ODHUE *Elmira*

Belvidere Mills

BELVIDERE

hue

*Goodhue
Centre*

Thoten ● *(Belvidere)*

ey

Crystal Springs

Bellechester

*White
Willow*

ZUMBROTA

*The Ghost Towns
& Discontinued Post Offices
of Goodhue County
(by township)*

Forest Mills

rota

Lena

60

● *Poplar Grove*

E ISLAND

Island

The

GHOST TOWNS

& Discontinued Post Offices of Goodhue County

Roy W. Meyer

Goodhue County Historical Society Press • Red Wing, Minnesota • 2003

Photo Source Abbreviations
GCHS from Goodhue County Historical Society
RWM from the personal collection of the author

On the Cover
Burkard's County Hotel at Hay Creek (see also page 61). *GCHS*
(Back cover) Roy W. Meyer, 1991. *RWM*

Map
The Ghost Towns & Discontinued Post Offices of Goodhue County. *RWM*

Frontispiece
Wanamingo town hall in Aspelund, 1941 (see also page 10). *RWM*

Editing, Design, Production
E. B. Green Editorial, St. Paul, Minnesota

Indexing
Patricia Green, Homer, Alaska

Printing
Sexton Printing, Inc., St. Paul

Binding
Muscle Bound Bindery, Minneapolis

Contents

Preface   viii

1. The Rural Post Office   3

2. The Surviving Post Offices   7

3. The Discontinued Post Offices and Ghost Towns   11

4. Some Concluding Observations   113

   References   117

   Sources   118

   Index   126

   About the Author   132

Preface

Ghost towns, especially those in Goodhue County, have interested me since 1939. One day in August of that year a traveling salesman appeared at our farm home and persuaded my mother to buy a copy of C. A. Rasmussen's *History of Goodhue County*. A few weeks earlier I had begun taking pictures of general stores, cheese factories, railroad depots, and other buildings in small villages that had not realized their founders' high hopes. The Rasmussen book, notably the page titled "Forgotten Cities," heightened my interest in such communities.

After some 15 years of continued but casual interest in ghost towns, I undertook in 1954 a serious piece of research—a detailed history of Forest Mills, based largely on backfiles of the *Zumbrota News*. This project eventuated in two published articles—one in the March 1956 issue of *Minnesota History* and another in *Zumbrota: The First 100 Years* (1956). In the early 1960s I began investigating two villages—Bombay and Skyberg—in the Kenyon area. Because Bombay had arrived late on the scene, early in the 20th century, county histories totally neglected it. I traced Bombay's history in some detail in an article published in the *Kenyon Leader* on April 29, 1965.

Nearly all of Goodhue County's ghost towns had post offices at one time, but many other rural post offices never achieved even the dignity of crossroads hamlets. In October 1963, at the end of a three-week bout of research in the National Archives on an unrelated subject, I spent half a day among the postal records, jotting down all I could find about the post offices that at one time existed in the county. The information there consisted mainly of the names of postmasters and dates of appointment; some records also listed the post-office locations.

Over the next four years I spent much of my leisure time paging through yellowed newspapers and consulting county records and other sources, recording virtually every scrap of information encountered about the vanished or declining villages. From time to time I also interviewed residents of these communities and collected data on their more recent histories. Eventually I had enough information to begin writing. When I had progressed some way into the project, I became aware that I was doing much more than summarizing the postal history of these places. I was telling the stories of the communities themselves. Thus my expanded title—*The Ghost Towns and Discontinued Post Offices of Goodhue County.*

By popular definition a *ghost town* is a place once of some importance that has declined greatly or disappeared. The mining districts of the West are dotted with the relics of towns that sprang up suddenly, flourished for a few exciting years, then as swiftly lost their populations, leaving empty buildings and grass-grown streets. In the Midwest, the process took longer, and buildings tended to disappear as a town declined; often, there is little visible evidence of a ghost town. The casual visitor may notice three or four houses where a larger community once thrived. Yet such a place is as much a ghost town as the popular tourist spots of Nevadaville and Tincup, Colorado, of South Pass City and Atlantic City, Wyoming, of Bannack and Elkhorn, Montana. In that midwestern sense, this work classifies such as ghost towns.

Let's also define the term *hamlet*. In a 1941 article on "The Unincorporated Hamlet," in the journal *Rural Sociology*, Glen T. Trewartha offered the following. A hamlet, he wrote, must have:

> a minimum of four active residence units, at least two of which are non-farm houses . . . Counting four and one-half people to a residence, this figure of at least four residence units in a hamlet establishes a minimum population of 18 or 20. Supplementary items of the definition stipulate a minimum of six active functional units, residential, business, social, or otherwise, and a total of at least five buildings actively used by human beings. These buildings must be spaced in such a way as to give an appearance of compactness exceeding that of ordinary farmstead spacing. In a hamlet composed of the minimum number of buildings, the maximum linear distance between the outermost buildings should not exceed one-quarter mile.

By the time of Trewartha's definition, many Goodhue County communities qualified as hamlets. Aspelund, Bellechester, Belle Creek, Belvidere Mills, Bombay, Claybank, Eggleston, Hader, Hay Creek, Roscoe, Skyberg, Sogn, Stanton, Vasa, Wacouta, Wangs, Wastedo, and White Rock all had had at least one general store. Bellechester, Belle Creek, Belvidere Mills, Fair Point, Hader,

Lena, Nansen, Roscoe, Roscoe Center, Skyberg, Sogn, Stanton, and Vasa had creameries or cheese factories. Most had rural schools, and a few had other businesses, churches, or town halls. Most had enough houses, including non-farm dwellings, to meet Trewartha's specifications.

Sixty years later, however, few of these could qualify as hamlets without substantial modification of the definition. All the rural schools were gone. All the creameries and cheese factories had closed their doors. And nearly all the general stores and other small businesses had joined them in oblivion. Only Hay Creek and White Rock could qualify as hamlets, the latter by the slimmest margin. The unincorporated post office villages of Frontenac and Welch came to meet the definition later. Bellechester, now incorporated, does not fit Trewartha's definition.

Yet most of these places, and others like Forest Mills (whose 12 houses are nearly all nonfarm dwellings), are clearly recognizable nodes of settlement, easily distinguished from scattered farmsteads nearby. If not hamlets, what are they? I propose a modified definition of *hamlet,* one more in keeping with contemporary reality. Retain the residential portion of Trewartha's definition, but delete the requirement of business or institutional buildings. Define *hamlet* as a place with a minimum of four occupied houses, including at least two non-farm dwellings, within a quarter mile of one another.

Some of the places treated here do not qualify under even this relaxed definition. There are simply not enough houses left in Aspelund, Belle Creek, Claybank, Fair Point, Holden, Lena, Nansen, Wangs, Wastedo, White Willow, and perhaps others for us to call them *hamlets.* But nearly all of them had post offices at one time, and they survived as trading centers long after the post offices were gone. On those grounds they merit inclusion with the places somewhat larger.

Despite the addition of *Ghost Towns* to my title, the county's discontinued post offices remained the central topic of my investigation. In places like Spring Creek or Miami or Finney, which never developed into hamlets, the post offices provided what little identity they had. Most of the places discussed here did, however, become at least country villages, only later declining from the size and importance they once enjoyed.

My original manuscript, completed in 1967, provided a great deal of information beyond that related to the post offices, including sketches of communities that never acquired post offices—such as Troy, Oxford Mills, Sevastopol, and two of the three Belle Creeks. I did not then include Barr, a hamlet that grew up around a clay plant in Minneola township, or Bombay in Cherry Grove. The latter still had three active business places in the 1960s and thus did not qualify as a ghost town. Here I include both of these for reasons that will become evident.

At one time or another, several other place names have appeared on maps of Goodhue County. Some were railroad stations (Bakko, Finseth Station, Fagen, Bellechester Junction, Stroms, Cannon Junction, West Red Wing, Trout Brook, Clay Pits, and Welch Station). Others were business places named for their owners (Harliss, or Harlistown, and Hartville) or rural neighborhoods (Spring Garden and Flower Valley). One, Mineral Springs, was both a tuberculosis sanatorium and a railroad station. Early Swedish settlers in Vasa township named their community Jemtland. One early map shows a place called Allandale, also in Vasa. An 1877 county map shows Wells Creek Mills in the eastern part of Hay Creek, crediting it with a blacksmith shop, a school, and a cemetery, as well as a country mill. None of these (or others like them) ever had a post office or developed into trading points; hence their exclusion from this study.

The space allotted here to each post office or ghost town is not necessarily proportionate to its relative importance or length of service. Some receive more extensive treatment than others simply because more information is available. But I have made a deliberate effort to rescue some post offices from near-oblivion. Aurland, Crystal Springs, and Miami had such brief careers or existed so long ago that information about them is hard to come by. I dug deep to find what is here. In other cases, such as Ayr or Fair Point, the community itself disappeared—thus the collections of minute information to reconstruct towns that once were.

This work draws from a variety of sources. Most of the post office data comes from the Registers of Appointments and Site Location Surveys, official Post Office Department documents now in the National Archives. Background information on the villages with post offices derives mainly from newspaper files and state and county gazetteers and directories. I have used county histories with caution. Goodhue County has been unusually productive of such histories, but the later ones, especially the ambitious Curtiss-Wedge volume, tend to be uncritical rehashes of their predecessors. Plat books and atlases, together with a miscellaneous collection of published sources, also were useful. Official county records, especially those in the Office of the County Recorder, have provided data, and the federal census schedules, especially those for 1860, 1870, and 1880, divulge personal data on persons too obscure to have appeared in the biographical sections of county histories. Finally, interviews, particularly for the recent past, have provided details otherwise unrecorded.

None of these sources is wholly free from error. County histories have a reputation for unreliability, and gazetteers are not much better. Because contemporary newspapers provide a kind of evidence unobtainable elsewhere, we are tempted to trust them more than they deserve. Their own corrections and retractions suggest further mistakes that no one bothered to bring to the editors' attention. With published materials composed from handwritten copy, printers and compositors had to guess at the spelling of proper names. Thus some names appear variously spelled. Newspapers often left the reporting of events outside the town of publication to "rural correspondents," who submitted items when they felt like it and in varying degrees of legibility. The reliance on handwritten copy means that even official records are not free of error, especially as to the spelling of names.

Although no amount of research can be exhaustive, mine has at least been extensive. I looked at nearly every surviving issue of every weekly newspaper published in the county before 1900 as well as a large selection of those published after that date. In addition, I consulted newspapers from neighboring counties for information on places located near the county line. For the other published and unpublished sources, my research has been not far from exhaustive. Still, I might have obtained more information on the recent past from additional interviews.

In the interests of readability, I do not burden the text with footnotes, which here would tend to repetition. In many cases, I mention sources within the text. Where no source is indicated, the reader may assume that names and dates of appointment of postmasters, for instance, come from official Post Office Department records and that background information comes from newspapers. A complete list of sources appears at the end of the text.

The Ghost Towns

and Discontinued Post Offices

of Goodhue County

1

The Rural Post Office

For nearly half a century after Goodhue County opened to white settlement, most of its people received mail at small rural post offices. Some of these were in farmhouses; more were located in country crossroads stores. In either case, local people traveled, sometimes from a considerable distance for pre-automobile days, to get their mail.

In 1870, more than 81 percent of Goodhue County's population (22,598) lived in the country or in unincorporated villages. By 1880 it was still more than 72 percent. As late as 1890, almost 64 percent of the population still lived outside the limits of the five places that were incorporated. The countryside then was densely settled compared with today's. Holden township had 1,199 inhabitants in 1870, compared with 466 a century later (and 445 in 1990). Wanamingo township had 1,468 in 1870, only 498 in 1970 (and 472 in 1990). Such a rural population required trading points at convenient locations; hence the numerous hamlets scattered about the countryside, with their general stores, blacksmiths, shoemakers, and the like. Hence also the many post offices.

The earliest post offices in Goodhue County—Red Wing, Westervelt (later Frontenac), and Central Point—were strung along the Mississippi River. Red Wing received its mail by riverboat during the season of navigation. The boats refused to stop at the other points, so star routes supplied them. (The name star route derives from the asterisk marking contracts for mail routes with no designated form of transportation.) As inland offices came into being along main avenues of travel or in settlements, star carriers supplied them, too. Besides the St. Paul and Dubuque road, established in 1854 and cutting across the county diagonally from northwest to southeast, star routes originated at Red

Wing, radiating to Faribault, Kenyon, Mantorville, and other points. Stage-coaches carried passengers as well as mail on these routes.

In April 1858 the Red Wing *Republican* reported that David Hancock had put a line of coaches on his mail route that would take passengers to Mantorville, Wasioja, Zumbrota, Owatonna, Oronoco, Rice Lake, Geneva, Albert Lea, and several other budding cities. Post offices were established on or near the star routes. If demand seemed great enough, a route might be changed to accommodate additional localities. Sometimes efforts towards new post offices failed. In 1859, an apparently fraudulent attempt to get a post office for "Mossville" came to naught.[1]

The coming of the railroads led to the establishment of some new post offices, but that did not mean the end of post offices off the rail lines. So long as a community needed a post office and could produce someone willing to act as postmaster—no one inquired deeply into qualifications—the community could retain its office. Post offices were established off the railroads even in the later 1890s, just before the appearance of rural free delivery (RFD).

Political preferment may have counted in the selection of postmasters, but the range of candidates usually did not allow much choice. The owner of the local store most often got the job and passed it on to the next owner. At one time two partners—one a Democrat, the other a Republican—ran the Roscoe store. No matter which party held sway in Washington, the post office stayed put.

There was not much money in the job of postmaster. Wayne E. Fuller remarked in his 1964 study of RFD that in 1899 no fourth-class postmaster made more than $1,000 a year from the business. The average annual salary was about $200. Still, there were obvious advantages to having the post office in one's store, and rural postmasters probably opposed changes to the system.

To people of the late 19th century, the rural post office must have seemed as permanent an institution as marriage. It had always existed, and it always would. Yet in just five years, 20 of the 34 Goodhue County post offices active in 1900 closed. This astonishing transformation of the local postal scene resulted from an experiment in Carroll County, Maryland, in 1899, when RFD routes replaced 63 of 94 fourth-class post offices. The innovation came to Goodhue County in the same year, with the establishment of two routes from Red Wing. From this beginning RFD expanded rapidly to the other larger offices in the county, and soon the need for the country post offices vanished.

Not all the post offices discussed here were victims of RFD. Many came and went before that innovation upset traditional arrangements. Some owed their demise to changes in transportation routes, others to a lack of anyone qualified to serve as postmaster. However stable the rural post office as an institution may have seemed, individual offices were temporary affairs, established to serve the populations of specific localities and always subject to change. Only village post offices could expect permanence. And even that expectation proved unwarranted when RFD emerged.

2

The Surviving Post Offices

While many of Goodhue County's early post offices fell by the wayside, others still function today. The earliest (by nearly five years) surviving post office is that at Red Wing, which, according to postal records, was established on August 6, 1850, as Wah-coo-ta, with F. T. Aiton postmaster. The postmaster's name is probably a mistake. The Rev. John Felix Aiton had come as a missionary in 1848 to the Dakota (Sioux) Indian village at the foot of Barn Bluff. Wacouta (or Wahkute), last in a line bearing the traditional name Red Wing, was chief. Aiton left the mission station before the post office was established. According to a later county history, the commencement of postal service was delayed until the following year, when the Rev. John W. Hancock, Aiton's fellow missionary, became its first postmaster, He traveled to St. Paul at his own expense to take the oath of office. Whatever the exact sequence of those events, postal records indicate that on October 7, 1850, two months after establishment of the Wah-coo-ta post office, its name was changed to Red Wing.

The second of the still-extant post offices is Frontenac, established as Westervelt on May 9, 1855, with Evert Westervelt (1816–1888) postmaster. The Westervelt office became Frontenac on January 18, 1860.

The first of the inland post offices was Cannon River Falls, established June 18, 1855, with James McGinnis postmaster. The official name persisted long after the town became generally known as Cannon Falls. Not until August 15, 1889, did the Post Office Department shorten the designation. Two surviving post offices opened in 1856—Pine Island on September 12 with John Chance postmaster, and Kenyon on December 18 with Samuel A. Barker postmaster. Two more opened in 1857—Zumbrota on June 15 with Thomas P.

Kellett postmaster, and Wanamingo on July 7 with James G. Brown postmaster. The original Wanamingo, which Brown had platted the same summer, was about a mile west of the present town. The newer Wanamingo sprang up in 1903 with construction of the Chicago, Milwaukee, St. Paul & Pacific Railway Company's branch line from Faribault to Zumbrota.

The other three post offices still existing are products of the 1880s. With the building of the Minnesota and Northwestern Railroad Company line in 1885 came a new town on the Goodhue-Rice county line. Named Dennison, it acquired a post office on December 4, 1885. Local storekeeper Gunder Bonhus was postmaster. On April 27 of the next year the Welch post office was established on the Cannon River in Welch township. The Eagle Mills post office had earlier operated in the vicinity, and now two railroads, one on each side of the river, provided an outlet for the products of the local mill. The first postmaster, Samuel Nelson, achieved an enviable record by retaining the office for more than 50 years. When the Duluth, Red Wing & Southern Railroad Company extended its line from Red Wing to Zumbrota in 1888–89, a new town was laid out in the southern part of Goodhue township. On September 21 the old Goodhue Centre post office moved to the new site with the new name Goodhue. The changes warrant its treatment as a separate office.

Wanamingo town hall in Aspelund, 1941. *RWM*

3

The Discontinued Post Offices
and Ghost Towns

Aspelund

The Aspelund post office, fourth in Wanamingo township, opened on February 6, 1872, with Christian Hveem (1835–1908) its first postmaster. Hveem was a veterinarian who later practiced medicine at Hader. An atlas published in 1874 shows the post office, erroneously called Ashland, in the northeast quarter of section 16, where Hveem resided. The name, which appears in both Norway and the Smaland district of Sweden, refers to a grove of aspens or poplars and reflects the heavily Norwegian settlement that began in the area about 1856.

In 1859 a group of settlers formed an association, at first exclusively religious in purpose. The Aspelund Society held an organizational meeting in the summer of 1862, during which it laid the foundations of the present Emmanuel Lutheran Church. In 1875, 40 farmers organized a mercantile association under that name and erected a store in the apex of the angle formed by roads coming from the north and northeast, near the southwest corner of section 16. The president of the association, Osmund J. Wing, became postmaster on April 28, 1875. The post office probably then relocated to the store or to Wing's residence on the south line of section 8. The first manager of the store is said to have been Augustinius Faehn. William A. Williamson had previously operated a general store on the south line of section 9, served by the Aspelund post office.

As a commercial enterprise the Aspelund Society was successful for a time but later dissolved. Then the store came into private ownership. On June 12, 1882, Peter A. Henning replaced Wing as postmaster. He retained the position until January 4, 1894, when Martin P. Heltne, then operating the store, succeeded him. In 1897, Heltne auctioned off his store and moved to Hayfield.

Aspelund store, 1939. *RWM*

Henning again took over the store. Reappointed postmaster on October 19 of that year, he retained the office for the rest of its life.

Aspelund was something of a trading center in the 1880s and 1890s. By 1882 it had a blacksmith, Henry Sands, and a flour-and-feed mill run by N. Norby. Two years later Nils Roland was operating the feed mill and a

Emmanuel Lutheran Church, Aspelund, 1954. *RWM*

second blacksmith shop. B. O. Norby had taken over the Sands shop. Late in 1888 the Crescent Creamery Company erected a creamery there. It had a brief career, but the feed mill was in business as late as 1896.

The coming of rural free delivery (RFD) soon after the turn of the century spelled the doom of most rural post offices, including Aspelund. An order to discontinue effective September 30, 1902, was rescinded because of no provision for delivery to its patrons. The Aspelund post office closed on January 14, 1905, a year or two after most of the other rural post offices in the county. Henning continued to operate the store until 1931, when he sold it to Hans Hjermstad. After running it for 15 years, Hjermstad sold it in 1946 to Lyle Hogstad, who in turn sold it to C. C. Matteson. He ran it until June 24, 1952, when a severe windstorm so damaged the old building that it was unsafe for occupancy. After standing vacant for a decade, it was torn down in the summer of 1962. All the other business places closed their doors many years earlier. Besides the new Wanamingo town hall, which replaces the original one, all that remains of the hamlet of Aspelund are three houses and the flourishing Emmanuel Lutheran Church.

Aurland

Aurland holds the record for brevity of life among Goodhue County post offices. Established May 5, 1898, it closed July 22 of the same year. Its first and only postmaster was John T. Wangen, whose farm home was in section 2, Warsaw township, on the hill west of today's Wangen Prairie Lutheran Church. According to Wangen's son, Carl J. Wangen, the post office operated in a cheese factory partway down the hill from the postmaster's house. The office received scant attention from contemporary newspapers. A one-sentence paragraph in the *Cannon Falls Beacon* announced its establishment (nearly a month late). A shorter notice of its closing appeared a few weeks later.

The name Aurland derives from Wangen's birthplace, noted in a biographical sketch as "Aurlands Vangen, Bergens Stift, Norway." Then the locality was commonly known as High Prairie. Since the building of the church in 1901 (dedication August 1902), however, it has become "Wangen Prairie."

The Crystal Creamery Company apparently started the Wangen (not to be confused with Wangs) cheese factory in June 1893 as a milk separator. In less than three months it closed, and its creditors settled for the building and machinery. After running a checkered course, the business finally got on its feet and in 1897 became a cheese factory. During the brief period in which it housed the post office, the factory thrived, undergoing $300 worth of improvements during the last nine months of 1898 and the first three months of 1899. The demand for cheese apparently was greater than the factory could meet.

Although it continued to operate after the turn of the century, by 1904 the cheese factory was in trouble. Someone wrote to the *Beacon* suggesting that the owners consider erecting a cheese factory or creamery at Oxford Mills, which the writer regarded as a more suitable location. The owners of the factory paid no heed. The *Beacon* reported that the patrons held a final meeting on September 30 of that year, but the factory apparently kept going, at least sporadically. On March 27, 1906, an auction of the building and its contents took place. The next week the newspaper announced, "The Wangen cheese factory is no more; it being discontinued preparatory to being moved away." Thus the Wangen cheese factory followed the Aurland post office to oblivion.

Ayr

The third post office in Cherry Grove township was Ayr, established on April 20, 1863, with Israel T. Comstock postmaster. Ayr is the name of a former county in Scotland, the home of poet Robert Burns. Some early settlers of the vicinity, such as David Simpson and Daniel C. Smith, were born in Scotland. They probably chose the name on this account. The history of the Ayr post office is especially muddled: it ceased operation once, reopened nearly ten years later, moved two or three times, and gave rise to no permanent village.

As with several other post offices in western Goodhue County, Ayr's early postmasters had British names, while many of the later ones were of Norwegian ancestry. Comstock, 58 at the time of the 1860 census, was born in New York. Carry (or Carey) D. Brown, another transplanted New Yorker, succeeded him on July 23, 1867. Henry Catlin, also a native of New York, followed Brown on November 24, 1868. Little more than a year later, on January 3, 1870, still another New Yorker, Solomon Sutherland (*Sunderland* in the postal records) replaced Catlin. Sutherland gave way on April 7, 1871, to Jacob N. Nesson, the first of the foreign-born postmasters at Ayr. All these men were farmers; Nesson also ran a small store.

The original site of the Ayr post office evidently was the southeast quarter of section 22, where Comstock had taken a claim in July 1857. An 1877 county map shows Comstock as owning land in the southwest quarter of section 23. The small "Comstock cemetery," now overgrown with weeds and sumac, is located there. During (and probably before) Sutherland's term, the post office was in the northwest corner of section 26. Such commercial activity as Ayr boasted then was concentrated at the crossroads where sections 22, 23, 26, and 27 meet. A gazetteer published in 1875 lists only one business place—Catlin & Brother, general store. By 1878, however, the firm of Bjorgo and Catteye (probably a misprint for Bergo and Catlin or Aabye) also operated a store there. Henry Catlin ran a blacksmith shop, and physician E. J. Winston listed Ayr as his address.

Meanwhile, the office changed hands four times. Harvey Catlin, younger brother of Henry, became postmaster on January 29, 1874. Newland Catlin followed on December 16, 1875, Daniel C. Smith on July 26, 1876, and John G.

Bjorgo (*Bergo* in postal records) on October 12, 1877. By 1880 the store had passed into the hands of Andrew L. Aabye, then 25, appointed postmaster on March 11. Although Aabye ran the store as late as 1884, three others had held the position of postmaster by that time. Israel T. Comstock (perhaps a son of the earlier postmaster of that name) began March 30, 1882. Mrs. Ellen M. Simpson replaced him on August 28, 1882. And Cortland D. Hunt, a native of Michigan then in his early forties, succeeded her on May 22, 1883. A gazetteer for 1884–85 lists Hunt as the proprietor of a general store, in addition to Aabye's store and Catlin's blacksmith shop.

There is no certainty that all three of these business places were at the crossroads or that the post office remained there through the many changes of postmaster. Further complicating the problem, several publications used the name Cherry Grove in referring to the locality served by the Ayr post office. An 1873 gazetteer lists "J. N. Nisson" as proprietor of a general store at Cherry Grove. Obviously, he was Jacob N. Nesson, postmaster at Ayr that year. A county history mentions Daniel C. Smith, also a postmaster at Ayr, as operating a store at Cherry Grove from 1871 to 1877.

Despite the abundance of experienced personnel, the Post Office Department could not find a successor to Cortland D. Hunt. So on February 4, 1884, the Ayr post office closed, and the Roscoe post office, three miles away, took on the community's postal service. Until 1893 the name Ayr was absent from the list of Goodhue County post offices. Then, on November 6, the office reopened—about a mile north of its original site—on the southeast corner of section 15. The new postmaster was James Simpson, who retained the office until it closed on September 30, 1902. According to a sketch map prepared by the Spring Creek postmaster in 1898, the Ayr post office was by then in the southwest corner of section 14.

Although there was a store at Ayr until 1898, the post office apparently was somewhere else. Early in 1896 Layng and Barsness took over the store, and late in 1898 the firm moved it to Skyberg. Upon its removal, the Cherry Grove correspondent for the *Red Wing Republican* commented, "All that now remains of the once thriving and prosperous village of Ayr is a hole in the ground." This doleful intelligence was not literally true, for the post office continued for nearly four years. With its demise, the last vestige of Ayr disappeared.

Bellechester
Bellechester is far from being a ghost town, but it qualifies as a discontinued post office. In fact, its postal facilities closed three times and reopened twice. At the end of the 20th century it was the largest community and the only incorporated city in Goodhue County without a post office—or even a postal station.

The original *Belle Chester* grew up in the 1870s on the border between Belvidere township in Goodhue County and Chester township in Wabasha

Bellechester Main Street, 1940. *RWM*

County. A frame structure, the original St. Mary's Church, was built in 1865 on the north side of the road marking the county line. A stone edifice replacing it in 1877 served the community until 1926, when a fire destroyed it. The present church went up later that year. Moved to a new site, the original church structure served as a school from 1881 until it was replaced by a large brick building in 1902. The school closed in 1968.

Business activity in Belle Chester began in 1871, when Nicholas Heber (or Hieber) started a general store and saloon, following it a few years later with a stone blacksmith shop and wagon shop that stood, in various capacities, until 1973. In 1877 Anthony M. Casper opened a general store across the road from the blacksmith shop, on the Wabasha County side. When a post office opened at Belle Chester, on April 30, 1879, Casper was its postmaster. He held the office until May 27, 1897, when his son, Joseph H. Casper, took over. The younger Casper remained postmaster until the post office closed on February 28, 1903, a casualty of RFD. Joseph Casper continued to run the store until 1938, when his son John took charge. John Casper sold it in 1942 to Joseph Poncelet. Other owners followed, but eventually the store closed, and part of the building was torn down.

Business places, most of them in Wabasha County, came and went in "Old Belle Chester," as the settlement came to be called after 1910. Another combination store and saloon opened in 1883, kitty-corner from Casper's store, in Goodhue County. It later burned, but other businesses succeeded it. In 1930 Walter and Leonard Arndt built a Standard Oil station on the site. It had several owners after 1971, and David Poncelet uses it now for a car-crushing business. About 1913, a hall went up across the road (west) from the Casper store, on or near the site of a tavern opened in 1909 by John B. Huberty. The Knights of Columbus Hall Association acquired the hall later and sold it to the City of Bellechester in 1996. To establish tax-exempt status for the building, the city leased it to the Bellechester Community Center Association, which uses it for a variety of activities.

"New Bellechester," a half-mile north of the old town, owes its existence to the discovery of a deposit of clay about 1910. In June of that year the Red Wing Sewer Pipe Company bought 160 acres east of the north-south road (now Goodhue County Highway 2) from Matt and Nick Strauss and began extracting clay. The Chicago Great Western Railway (CGW) built a branch from near Goodhue with company labor and platted a new town, recorded on October 22. After an auction of lots held November 3, a boardinghouse of 70 by 45 feet was built to accommodate workers. A complete line of business places opened its doors late that year and through 1911. The *Mazeppa Journal* remarked that something "very rare in these old settled parts of Minnesota . . . A boom town is springing up."[2]

By May 12, 1911, the *Journal* could report that the Red Wing Malting Company had erected a grain elevator, the Betcher Lumber Company had put up an office and several large sheds, and the Farmers State Bank had built a modest brick structure, nearly ready for business. Albert Burkard (no apparent relation to the Hay Creek Burkhards) had started a saloon, which some claim was the first business place in New Bellechester. Still in operation after many changes of ownership, what is now Counter's Bar claims some longevity. Also in 1911 Frank Strauss and two of his brothers opened a general store on the west side of Main Street. Frank ran the place alone from 1916 to 1952; his son Clem bought and continued operating the store, then closed it in 1963. A hardware and implement store nearly across the street from the Strauss store underwent several changes before it became a general store in 1931, when Wilfred Majerus took charge. Closed in the mid-1980s, the building then was torn down.

Bellechester continued to grow for several years after 1911. A blacksmith shop appeared in 1912, a feed mill in 1913, a coal business and a meat market sometime in the same decade, the Bellechester Cooperative Creamery in 1914, and the Bellechester Garage in 1919. J. B. Majerus and his son Richard, who bought an earlier garage building from Nick Strauss, ran the garage. Other businesses doubtless led short lives there, leaving few memories. At one time there were a coal business west of the elevator, a stockyard nearby, a second hardware store north of the Strauss store, and, in 1926, three blacksmith shops. During this halcyon era, Bellechester's second post office enjoyed its six-year career. Postal records give the date of establishment as January 24, 1911, but local newspapers reported its opening on August 1. The first postmaster was

Willis R. Sawyer, cashier at the bank, who kept the office in the bank building. Frank M. Strauss succeeded him on January 2, 1917, and he doubtless moved the post office to his general store. It closed the following May 15.

The end of the post office may have been an augury, but Bellechester prospered several more years. The first boardinghouse burned in 1922, and a new one went up to serve as long as the clay-digging operation continued. In 1923 the Goodhue County Cooperative erected a two-story stucco building. There a general merchandise and hardware store operated for a decade or more. A large frame public school, built just north of town in the early 1920s, served until the 1950s, when it closed before the general consolidation of rural schools.

Thus by the 1920s, Bellechester, if not the "thriving little city" predicted by the *Goodhue Enterprise* in 1910, was at least a trading center for a prosperous farming area. To a considerable extent, however, it depended on the clay industry that had brought it into being. The shutdown of that industry in July 1924 led to the closing of most of the business places then existing. In 1910 there had appeared to be enough clay for 20 years of mining. While that estimate may have been technically correct, in the early 1920s the only clay lay so deep that mining it was no longer feasible.

When the taverns and other businesses of Bellechester lost the trade of the 60 or 70 men once employed in the clay pits, their situation became precarious. Of the major enterprises in the village, the bank was the first to go. Started in 1911 with a capital and surplus of $13,500, it managed to survive until the Great Depression. Closed along with other banks in the Bank Holiday of 1933, it consolidated with the Goodhue State Bank the following year. The building, used successively for offices and a restaurant, passed from hand to hand. Then the American Legion, still the owner today, took it over.

The big co-op store closed a year or two later. Its new owner used it for a time as a tavern, holding roller-skating and dances and showing movies from time to time. In 1958 the Du Lac Company purchased it with plans for a picture-framing business employing 20 people, with an annual payroll of more than $60,000. But the business languished, the owner vanished one night, and the building stood empty until it was razed.

Bellechester was quiet by 1940, when the author rode his bicycle down Main Street one hot August day. He noted that the proprietors of the two general stores could sit on their front steps and converse with each other without much interference from passing traffic. The town was by no means dead, however. Most of the businesses alive when the clay digging ended were still active—or others had replaced them. And there was one advance: on December 30, 1930, a rural station tributary to the Goodhue post office opened. For the first time since 1917, Bellechester citizens could buy stamps, money orders, and other postal materials and send letters bearing the Bellechester postmark. Like the earlier post office in its last days, the rural station operated in the Strauss store until it shut down on April 20, 1963, about the time Clem closed the store.

Although some businesses undoubtedly closed their doors without leaving public records, 14 still operated in August 1954, when the author took inventory. Old Bellechester had the Corner Grocery (the former Casper store), a Standard Oil station, and a tavern called Nick's Place. The other 11, all in New Bellechester, were the Bellechester Cooperative Creamery, the Commander Elevator, the Wedge Lumber Yard, N. H. Befort's blacksmith shop, the Strauss grocery, the Majerus grocery, the Corner (the American Legion hall, formerly a bank), Haas's Bar, Coonie's Place (now Counter's Bar), the Majerus garage, and a hardware store. Nick Strauss had started the hardware store that Adam Poncelet acquired about 1936. In 1931 Poncelet had taken over the coal business established by Joseph Conrad about 1911. The coal business perished when fuel oil replaced coal for home heating. Poncelet operated the hardware store until 1966, then sold it to Eldon Miller, who closed it about a year later.

Including the hardware store, Bellechester lost three major businesses in the late 1960s and early 1970s. The lumberyard established in May 1911 underwent several changes of ownership over the years. Lampert Yards operated it for a time. Its last owner, the Wedge Lumber Company of Zumbrota, closed it in 1969. A more serious loss was the closing of the creamery. Its importance had increased as the village turned more and more towards serving area farmers, and it enjoyed many prosperous years. The creamery appeared to be doing well when it observed its 50th anniversary in 1964. But by that time many small creameries and cheese factories were closing or consolidating with larger concerns. In 1972 the Bellechester Co-op agreed to merge with Land O'Lakes, on condition that the creamery stay in operation. After only six months, however, the new owners closed it down and moved its operations to Oak Center. After it stood empty for some 18 months, Marlin and Oryen Benrud purchased the building and there ran a feed-and-farm-supply business for the next 22 years. From 1996, the business continued under different ownership.

The grain elevator also endures. Operated for years by the Fleischmann Malting Company and later by Commander Elevators, it was acquired in 1982 by Farmers Elevator, which merged with AG Partners in 1996. The old elevator had been torn down the previous year; nine new grain bins, a new drying system, and an anhydrous ammonia plant replaced it. Among the other businesses still apparently thriving is the Bellechester Garage, since 1976 known officially as the Majerus Garage and Oil Company. In 1995 it expanded onto the site of the former Majerus store. For nearly 20 years Bellechester has again enjoyed the services of a bank. The Goodhue State Bank opened a branch there in 1981. When the Goodhue bank merged with White Rock State Bank, the Bellechester branch became part of the White Rock bank, resulting in an extraordinary situation—a bank in one town without a post office, with a branch in another town without a post office, either.

Although the number of business places in Bellechester unquestionably diminished after peaking in the early 1920s, its public spirit persisted and even increased. This trend became evident with a move in the mid-1950s to incorporate the community. On October 3, 1955, an election resulted in a five-to-one margin for incorporation as a fourth-class city. At a subsequent election, on October 27, voters chose Adam Poncelet mayor. Since then Bellechester has acquired the infrastructure expected of a city of its size, including a water system, a sewage disposal system, an expanded streetlight system, and some new streets with curbs and gutters.

The 1960 census, the first after incorporation, gave Bellechester a population of 184—131 in Goodhue County, 53 in Wabasha County. By 1970 this increased to 199, and by 1980 to 220—157 in Goodhue County, 63 in Wabasha. The 1990 census appeared to show a 50 percent loss—110 in Goodhue County and none at all in Wabasha! To anyone familiar with Bellechester, anyone aware of the houses going up there in recent decades, the figures made no sense. A revised count credited the city with 146—an improvement but still a decided drop from the 220 found there in 1980. As young people left for employment elsewhere and the total population aged, Bellechester may have lost some population after 1980, but a one-third decline in ten years seemed unlikely. The 1995 state census gave Bellechester 154 residents.

Besides sustaining church, veteran, and other community organizations, Bellechester revealed its public spirit by issuing a history titled *Memories of Bellechester,* early in the year 2000. (Much of the information in this sketch is from that book.) Despite an evident decrease in the number of business places and a probable decline in population, Bellechester still serves its rural community. It also provides homes for people employed in Red Wing and Rochester, for instance—part of the double role played by many small midwestern towns today.

Belle Creek
After the closing of the Burr Oak Springs post office in 1857, Belle Creek township was without an office for more than three years. Then, on June 16, 1860, Samuel P. Chandler became postmaster at a new office named Belle Creek in the northwest quarter of section 20. Chandler was an early settler in the township. His house served as a hotel for farmers from the western part of the county hauling wheat to Red Wing. After authorization of a post road from Red Wing to Faribault in 1864, Chandler's way station gained added patronage. A substantial stone building, it still stands after many years of service as a farmhouse. About 1865, Chandler, originally a Methodist, began conducting services as a lay reader in the Episcopal church; later he was ordained. Chiefly through his efforts, St. Paul's Episcopal Church, on a hill east of the hotel, was dedicated on June 26, 1873. The Chandler family is now rehabilitating the church.

Belle Creek Episcopal Church, 1953, host to a recent Chandler wedding. *RWM*

On October 16, 1874, David Schwieger replaced Chandler as postmaster. The post office closed the following December 9 but reopened November 9, 1875, with Charles F. Lindholm postmaster. A little more than a year later, on January 29, 1877, William J. Rice, who was running a general store at the time, replaced Lindholm. Betsy Chandler, daughter of the pastor, succeeded Rice on October 14, 1878. On May 9, 1881, A. W. Petersdorf replaced her. Petersdorf remained postmaster until the office closed January 9, 1882.

For several years the post office and church constituted the nucleus of a busy hamlet. An 1878 gazetteer listed a blacksmith shop, a harness shop, and a boot-and-shoe shop, in addition to Rice's general store. According to an 1877 county map, all were west of the road and south of the old hotel. The harnessmaker, Thomas Schwieger, was also a dealer in agricultural implements. A similar 1880 gazetteer, however, reported that no business was carried on at Belle Creek. With the closing of the post office in 1882, Belle Creek vanished from the gazetteers. The construction of the Minnesota Central railroad in 1882 took away much of its importance as a way station. Until 1940, if not later, an unused Independent Order of Good Templars (IOGT) hall stood on the hillside west of the road. The old church, unused since the early 1930s, still keeps vigil on the hill to the east.

Three communities bear the name of Belle Creek in Goodhue County. The one discussed above was the first. Prentiss M. Clark of Minneapolis platted the second, a "paper city," on May 7, 1883, in the east half of the southwest quarter of section 27, township 113, range 16. This was at the extreme northern end of Vasa township, on the line of the recently built Minnesota Central (later part of the CGW) across the Cannon River from today's village of Welch. Although platted in ambitious proportions, this Belle Creek apparently did not develop much beyond a theoretical stage. In November 1899 a depot erected there was moved a few rods west on two flatcars, to be renamed Welch for the village across the river. For many years the old building stood beside the tracks, the paint slowly flaking to reveal the earlier name, "Belle Creek." The railroad eventually razed the depot, then in 1982 was itself abandoned. The Joint Powers Board (Goodhue County, Cannon Falls, and Red Wing) acquired the right-of-way and constructed the present Cannon Valley Trail passing through the site of the second Belle Creek.

The third Belle Creek is the present trading point in section 8 of Belle Creek township. This 20th-century development dates from 1901, when A. V. Anderson led a group of farmers in deciding to establish a dairy cooperative. The Belle Creek Cooperative Creamery Company was organized in January 1902. Later that year it erected a frame building on what was later the parking lot of the Belle Creek Gardens. The creamery began operation the next July. Two years later the Belle Creek Mercantile Cooperative Company organized, then built a general store a short way south of the creamery. E. N. Anderson, formerly of Kenyon, was the first manager. Iver Bundlie succeeded him in 1907 but resigned four years later. Edmund Berg ran it until 1915, when he bought the Santleman store at Claybank. Subsequently the Belle Creek store passed into private ownership. For some years Richard McCardle operated it.

In 1920 the creamery co-op reorganized, and soon afterwards a masonry structure across the road replaced the by-then-inadequate building. The firm's growth was impressive. By 1930 it was selling 84,000 pounds of butter a year; by 1940 it sold 215,000 pounds. In line with the growing trend toward consolidation, however, the Belle Creek plant in 1952 affiliated with the Webster Cooperative Dairy Association. Thereafter the plant marketed its milk through that co-op. In 1958 Belle Creek shipped milk worth $368,679 to the Webster plant. Subsequently the Belle Creek plant ceased to collect milk and went into the feed-and-fertilizer business.

Though only a mile and a half from White Rock, this third Belle Creek retains its identity. Besides the creamery and the general store, long operated by Donald T. Garrison, it included for a time the Belle Creek Gardens, a roller-skating rink run in connection with the store, and two houses. The roller rink is still there, and though its stock now runs heavily to junk food, the store, almost the last of its kind in the county, also has survived. Clustered about the junction of Goodhue County Highway 8 and a Belle Creek township road, the settlement overlooks the valley of the stream that named three communities— and a township to boot.

Belvidere

A post office named Belvidere opened in the township of that name on January 24, 1878, with Anthon B. Jenson postmaster. Presumably because of confusion with the office of Belvidere Mills established the previous year, its name changed to Thoten on March 18, less than two months after its establishment. For further information, see Thoten (page 93).

Belvidere Mills

Though Goodhue County is not so known for milling as areas more south and east, at least four post offices, now closed, were established in the villages or hamlets growing up around rural flour mills. One of these was Belvidere Mills, in the northeast quarter of section 5, Belvidere township. As early as 1858, Nelson B. Gaylord, one of the first settlers there, used a hand-operated coffee mill to grind wheat for the convenience of his neighbors, who otherwise would have had to haul their grain some distance to make flour. After wearing out two or three such mills, he built in 1861 a gristmill powered by the flow of Wells Creek, then a much larger stream than it is today.

As the years passed, Gaylord's enterprise expanded. The industrial census of 1870 described the mill as having two run of stone and generating 18 horse-

Belvidere Mills post office. *GCHS*

power. Gaylord's investment showed up as $2,000. The value of the wheat ground during the previous year was $8,570. Still the county's smallest (of those listed in the census), the Belvidere mill filled an important place in the rural economy of the time. Gaylord, born in Pennsylvania in 1823, was sole proprietor of the mill and the hamlet that developed around it. He opened a general store as an adjunct to the mill. On September 28, 1877, he became postmaster at the new office of Belvidere Mills.

Gazetteers do not suggest much of a settlement at Belvidere Mills at that time. In 1878 the hamlet had 28 residents, a church (the German Methodist, a couple of miles east), and a rural school, in addition to Gaylord's mill and store. Two years later O. C. Oleson ran a blacksmith shop there, but by 1882 his name was gone. Still, a blacksmith shop operated at Belvidere Mills for many years. N. G. (Hy) Gibson ran it early in the 20th century just south of the present store.

Apparently the only other business started there was a creamery. Although 1893 and 1894 newspapers mention a "Belvidere cooperative creamery" with 65 patrons, they seem to refer to the ancestor of the Bellechester co-op creamery rather than to a concern at Belvidere Mills. Residents interviewed in the 1960s did not remember any creamery before 1911 when the Belvidere Cooperative was organized, though the Hammer creamery of Zumbrota collected milk from farmers in earlier years. On April 22, 1911, the cooperative filed its articles of incorporation, and soon it erected a substantial building along the main road somewhat east of the store. It opened for business on June 1. With later additions, it served local farmers until 1940, when it merged with the Lake City creamery. The county later acquired the building and converted it into a garage for the highway department.

Meanwhile, other changes occurred in Belvidere Mills. Gaylord had turned the store over to Fred Thomforde, and in 1897 Axel Ahlgren and Henry J. Bang took charge. Gaylord remained postmaster until January 26, 1904, when Bang succeeded him. Ahlgren left the community in 1910, leaving Bang to run the store by himself. The Belvidere Mills post office closed before that, on January 24, 1905. It was one of the last in the county to give way to RFD.

The mill continued operating, in its later years grinding feed only for local farmers. The old frame building was torn down some time after 1911, after a farmer living upstream sued owners John and William Diercks for building two brush dams, thus raising the water lever and flooding his land. The blacksmith shop was out of business by 1919, but Belvidere Mills's general store continued for many years. In 1914 Bang replaced the original building with a tile structure across the road. He moved into it in January of the next year. There he conducted his general merchandise business until 1939. About a year later, Arthur Diercks reopened the building as a tavern, where he also sold a few groceries. Because of a shortage of help during World War II, Diercks closed it in the summer of 1942, bringing to an end more than 80 years of business activity at Belvidere Mills. A community hall built about 1911, long used for dances and farmers' meetings, was torn down in 1948. Its lumber went to build a house nearby.

Belvidere Mills today consists of nine houses (some of them new), the former creamery building, and the old store, now a machine shed. The hamlet has always been off the main routes of travel, and the recent rerouting of Goodhue County Highway 3 isolates it even more. A sign along Trunk Highway (T.H.) 58 points to Belvidere Mills, but the traveler who turns onto the county road stands a good chance of missing the community altogether. The rural milling industry had a brief day of prosperity in Goodhue County, and when that day was over, settlements like Belvidere Mills entered upon a much longer period of decay, ending in virtual oblivion.

Black Oak

Black Oak was a short-lived post office on the east line of section 12, Belle Creek township, along an alternate route of the old Red Wing-to-Kenyon road. Established April 25, 1877, in the general store of Rosing and Doyle, it closed on February 10, 1885, reportedly because no one wanted to serve. Its first and only postmaster, Orvar G. Rosing, was born in Sweden about 1854. He settled in Goodhue County and began farming before opening his store at Black Oak.

The area served by the post office included several other business places. The *Minnesota State Gazetteer* for 1878–79 lists a blacksmith shop. The 1880–81 gazetteer adds another general store and a marble worker. By 1882 Philip Ryan apparently dealt in boots and shoes. Since that year he became postmaster at the new office of Ryan, his establishment must have been there rather than at Black Oak. Rosing and Doyle suffered more than one instance of theft. In 1879, after a robbery only two or three months earlier, the *Cannon Falls Beacon* reported S40 dollars' worth of postage stamps stolen. The store building, long since converted to a residence, stood many years. Someone finally tore it down, leaving no trace of Black Oak.

Bombay

Bombay, started in 1903, is the only entirely new village founded in Goodhue County in the 20th century. The present towns of Bellechester and Wanamingo are relocations of long-existing communities. Bombay, like the "new" Wanamingo, came into existence as a result of the last major railroad construction in the county, the Milwaukee extension from Zumbrota to Faribault.

From the time the Minnesota Midland (later part of the Milwaukee) built its narrow-gauge line from Wabasha to Zumbrota in 1878, there was talk of broadening the gauge and extending the track to Faribault. Twenty-five years later, the talk turned to action. Following surveys conducted late in 1901, much of the line was graded. After track was laid in 1903, the line opened to both

Bombay depot, 1941. *RWM*

freight and passenger traffic. Besides erecting a depot in Kenyon, the railroad company chose sites for four new stations. Two of these were in Rice County; Ruskin and Epsom soon had grain elevators. One was about a mile east of the crossroads village of Wanamingo, which had had a post office since 1857. Over the years a mill, a general store, and a creamery had grown up on the line between Wanamingo and Minneola townships. Now the railroad platted a town there, with lots going on sale April 24, 1903. The fourth station was to be about four miles east of Kenyon, on John Davidson's farm. As early as December 1901, when the survey was complete, Davidson, less than pleased at the prospect of a railroad track just south of his barn, threatened—facetiously, we assume—to lay out a townsite on his land and call it "Johnstown."

The L. M. Loomis Company of Minneapolis proposed building a grain elevator near the depot. Not long afterward, the Milwaukee Elevator Company announced that it, too, would build an elevator there. Both did build, and both began taking in grain late in 1903, about the time the new railroad line went into service. The next spring John H. Otterness and the Charlson brothers, Marcus and Jonas, who had conducted business at Sogn, opened a general store in Bombay, about ten rods north of the Loomis elevator. Farmers were talking about starting a cheese factory, but that proposal did not materialize until several years later.

When the railroad named its new station Bombay, some local people objected. The *Kenyon Leader* suggested naming it "Davidson," remarking that anything with a *son* in it would have more appeal in that Norwegian community than "some old thing from British India." In September 1903 a large number of farmers reportedly signed a petition to change the name to "Davidson" or "Spring Creek." The latter was the name of a rural post office in Cherry Grove township that had closed October 1 of the previous year.

Nothing came of the petition, and before long people became reconciled to the railroad's choice of depot name. No one ever advanced a convincing explanation for the choice. Perhaps some railroad official had come from Bombay, New York, a small town near the Canadian border. Or someone looking at a map of India may have chosen the name at random. Whatever the explanation, the name soon gained acceptance, taking its place alongside such other exotic place names in southern Minnesota as Berne, Cordova, Genoa, Geneva, Heidelberg, London, Potsdam, Warsaw, and—the most exotic—Eden.

Unlike the 24-by-60-foot depots at Wanamingo and Ruskin, the first one at Bombay was only a small freight shed. By August 1904, however, the new town was booming so vigorously that the railroad announced it would replace the shed with a depot 16 by 36 feet at the base and 14 feet high. There would be an office and waiting room on the west end, express and freight storerooms in the rest. Charlson Brothers & Otterness handled the freight business there for a time.

With the two elevators apparently thriving, local farmers became interested in forming a cooperative to buy one or both of them. Negotiations with the elevator companies, begun in 1906, went nowhere then or in the two following years. But early in 1909 several farmers formed an association and bought the Loomis elevator. The Bombay Farmers Mercantile and Elevator Company, organized April 22 with a capital of $10,000, made O. J. Wing its first president, R. H. Wickum vice president, Helmer Voxland secretary, and John Davidson treasurer. Before the end of the year the co-op also purchased the Milwaukee elevator (including a lumberyard). The two elevators, some distance apart, made for some inconvenience, but in 1916 the one to the east was moved to a new foundation adjacent to the other.

The year 1909 also brought to fruition the scheme of building a cheese factory at Bombay. During its first four years, Dave Kunz, a Pine Island cheesemaker instrumental in its start, operated the factory. Later the firm of Scherz and Heigle ran it. Early in 1913, however, a group of farmers, including several organizers of the elevator cooperative, purchased the factory and organized the Bombay Dairy Company, capitalized at $3,000. Despite a favorable picture of its operations in the *Leader,* the cheese factory seems never to have been very profitable. It closed about 1920.

Meanwhile, there were other changes in Bombay. In 1908 John Otterness bought out his partners, the Charlson brothers, to run the store by himself the next four years. In April 1912 he turned it over to Michael J. Davidson, son of John Davidson and one of the incorporators of the Bombay Dairy Company.

Though various people operated the store in the years following, it remained thereafter in possession of the Davidson family. In 1913 the Wanamingo firm of Swanson & Roe bought the lumberyard, and Charles O. Roe came to manage it, along with the elevator.

Bombay probably reached its peak about the time of World War I; it began a decline soon after the war. In 1919 the elevator changed its articles of incorporation to permit William Shepard of Kenyon to own more than the 20 shares of stock originally stipulated as the maximum per stockholder. After Shepard gained control of the company, his son Frank continued as manager for as long as the association existed. But in 1924 it became known that the elevator company, unable to meet its obligations, had suspended operations. Fleischmann Malting Company of Red Wing would buy it, keeping its management local. When the Shepards transferred their activities to Skyberg, Martin J. Ruud succeeded the younger Shepard as manager. Ruud, with his son Arnold, also ran the store. With a daughter, Mabel, clerking there, the Ruuds had a near-monopoly on Bombay's business.

When the cheese factory closed down, the building was sold, and Ole Yngsdal opened a garage in it in 1923. He ran it until 1939, when his brother Elmer took it over, continuing until the garage went out of business. The building was torn down in 1997.

In 1927 Carl Langness took over management of the Bombay store, and his wife, Signora, and her sister-in-law ran it for the next three years. With the start of the Great Depression, however, business no longer boomed, and in 1930 the store closed, its stock sold at a 10 percent discount. That same year, as railroads everywhere retrenched, agency service at the Bombay depot was suspended. D. D. Day, agent for about 15 years, apparently stayed on as custodian. Social news reports from the Bombay neighborhood included mention of him and his family for some time thereafter.

Despite economic blows suffered in the 1920s and early 1930s, Bombay was far from finished. In the summer of 1932 the state highway between Faribault and Zumbrota (then numbered T.H. 21, running a mile south of Bombay) was rerouted to pass by the Bombay store. The increase in traffic led Michael Davidson, who had inherited the store from his father on the latter's death in 1930, to put in a stock of groceries and reopen it. From that time almost until its closing in 1992, the Davidson family operated the store. Claremont and Esther Skillestad ran the business during its last years.

The elevator underwent further changes of ownership. In 1944 Fleischmann sold it to the Commander Elevator Company of Minneapolis, a division of Archer Daniels Midland (ADM). The Farmers Union Grain Terminal Association acquired the elevator in 1960, operated it until 1990, then sold it to Steve and Bruce Boyum, who run it now. Occasional improvements have kept the elevator abreast of changes in the business, and it continues to serve local farmers. The depot still stood in 1941 (see page 26); later only a sign along the tracks replaced it. When in 1979 the Milwaukee line abandoned its Zumbrota branch, Bombay lost the railroad that had spawned it.

The elevator is the only business remaining in Bombay, which also contains five houses (including the former store). Since it never had a church, school, or town hall, no institutional buildings survive to give it an identity of its own. Signs along the highway, now T.H. 60, announce Bombay to motorists, however, and so long as the elevator operates and a few people live there, the community will not be a ghost town. Founded close to the advent of RFD, Bombay never had a post office.

Burley

The Burley post office, in the southwestern part of Featherstone township, section 29, near the junction of today's county highways 1 and 6, had a short career. Established on June 29, 1897, with Clara G. Mix postmaster, it closed August 15, 1900, upon abandonment of the Red Wing-Kenyon stage route. Ezekiel Burleigh (or Burley) briefly kept a tavern there some 30 years earlier. His name apparently stuck.

Long before the opening of the Burley post office, local farmers built a schoolhouse of some architectural pretension. On February 28, 1874, David Hutcheson moved, and Burley seconded, that the school district (#115) build a brick school 26 by 42 feet and 14 feet high. The vote was yes; a bond issue

Burley school, Featherstone township, 1953. *RWM*

paid part of the cost, apparently only $3,000. The Burley school, with its library of 500 books, came to be a leader in rural education. It was one of the first country schools in the county to provide free textbooks.

The school closed in 1953, and the Dosdall Implement business across the road took it for a machine shed. The old school, the implement store (now Earl's Repair), and two or three houses now mark the spot, but the name of Burley is largely forgotten.

Burr Oak Springs

One of the earliest inland post offices in the county, Burr Oak Springs opened on June 18, 1855, with Henry M. Doyle postmaster. Cannon River Falls, established on the same date, Poplar Grove following in October, and Burr Oak Springs were the only Goodhue post offices outside the immediate Mississippi River valley before 1856. The three were on the route of the St. Paul and Dubuque stage line. Burr Oak Springs supposedly was in one of the northern-tier sections of Belle Creek township, where Walter Doyle and his five sons, including Henry, settled shortly after the territory opened to white settlement. The first claim recorded by a member of the family at the Red Wing land office (December 16, 1856) was that of Michael Doyle. He settled on the northwest quarter of section 3. Others of the family later made adjoining claims in sections 3 and 4. The Doyle cabin became a stopping point for travelers in 1854, and in 1855 such men as Henry Hastings Sibley, Alexander Ramsey, and Ojibway chief Hole-in-the-Day reportedly patronized it.

The earliest history of Goodhue County, published in 1869, erroneously dates the establishment of this post office (which it calls Burr Oak) to 1854 and states that it closed the following year upon a change in the stage route. Undoubtedly the more direct line from Cannon Falls to Oronoco left Doyle's way station isolated, but the post office remained until April 8, 1857. It was the first county post office to close down. When the Black Oak post office opened 20 years later, its name echoed this early inland office.

One of the least-known "paper cities" of Goodhue County, Troy (or Troy City), located near the Burr Oak Springs post office, may be regarded as its successor though it never had a post office itself.[3] The plat of Troy, surveyed in July 1857, presents some perplexing problems. Mitchell, in his 1869 county history, named James Allen the proprietor. Allen's name does appear on the plat, along with that of James W. Parker. Above their names is the word *witness.* The inscription at the top of the plat reads: "I the proprietor of the town of Troy do hereby certify that I caused the same to be laid out in town lots as here surveyed and platted and do hereby give the streets and alleys designated therein for public use." Philander Vandenburgh appears to have signed it. The singular "I" and other references suggests that Vandenburgh, not Allen and Parker, was proprietor. None of the three apparently stayed long in the county.

Smaller than most of the other towns platted that year, Troy covered only 40 acres. It had seven streets and 16 blocks, some of them fractional. Although the plat, recorded on July 21, gives no indication of the location, it appears to have been the northwest quarter of the southwest quarter of section 2, Belle Creek township, where Jesse A. Johnson made a claim in April 1856. If this is indeed the site, one wonders how familiar the proprietor was with the terrain. A north-facing escarpment cuts across the tract, with ravines extending back into the escarpment. This results in respectable bluffs. The surveyor, apparently S. A. Hart, probably knew the site well enough. The plat shows "springs" approximately where the U.S. Geological Survey (Goodhue West quadrangle, 1968) indicates a farm pond.

According to the Mitchell history, only one building ever existed at Troy. Johnson built a store there, stocked it with merchandise, and promptly closed it as a result of the economic depression following the Panic of 1857. Troy did not utterly disappear, however, for Joseph S. Sewall's 1857 map shows it in section 2, along the route of the Red Wing-Kenyon stage line. A delinquent tax list published in 1863 includes the entire plat of Troy but lists no owner. Whoever it was probably vacated the plat soon thereafter.

Cannon Valley

Cannon Valley was another post office of brief duration. Established on October 12, 1874, it closed July 5, 1877. The postmaster during its less-than-three-year life was Marcus J. Westby (*Weiby* in postal records). Scanty evidence of its location points to the eastern part of section 25, Warsaw township. By 1894 what was known as the "Cannon Valley Stock Farm" operated there; its name retained the reference to Cannon Valley past the turn of the century.

Cascade

The Cascade post office served a milling town in the extreme northwestern corner of Stanton township, on the Cannon River. Perhaps because of its location on the edge of the county and its orientation towards Rice and Dakota counties, Cascade received little attention from county historians. And county newspapers mentioned it less than its importance suggests.

Cascade had its origins in the Granville mills, erected in the 1860s. The first contemporary reference reports that Ephron Lockwood sold a half-interest in the mill to E[dmund] S. Bailey in August 1866. Two years later, in July 1868, Bailey and Samuel Collins apparently sold a half-interest to John A. Whitson. The 1869 Mitchell history makes passing reference to the Bailey & Collins mill on the Big Cannon River, but the 1870 Industrial Census includes the firm of Whitson & Byrnes, owners of a three-run mill representing an investment of $35,000. Generating 45 horsepower, the mill had an annual output of 13,000 barrels of flour. John Whitson, then 46, was a native of Scotland, as was his brother, William, eight years younger. John and Thomas "Burns" (Byrnes), ages 35 and 30, were natives of Ireland. The younger Whitson and Herman Metz, a Prussian immigrant of 40 years, were coopers. Another Irishman, John Keyes, was a blacksmith. Two teamsters belonged to the household of John Whitson, who evidently was head of the firm.

Not much more is known of the pre-1882 Granville mills. The Andreas atlas (1874) gives the location, but its historical sketch of Goodhue County confuses the Granville with the Oxford mills, built in 1867 on section 25 of Stanton township (see pages 36–37). The *Rice County Journal* (Northfield) occasionally mentions "Granville" or "Granville Mills." In 1880, for instance, a flash flood swept away the pontoon bridge across the Cannon River. The event that transformed the country mill into a thriving village, however, was the construction in 1882 of the two railroad lines up the Cannon valley from Red Wing to Northfield. The Minnesota Central, later absorbed by the CGW, opened for traffic December 20. The Chicago, Milwaukee & St. Paul Railway Company opened its line the following June 13. Both passed north of the river, in Dakota County, and both established stations named Granville Mills. The Minnesota Central reported 211 departures and 237 arrivals, amounting to $62.12 in passenger revenue in 1883. The Milwaukee reported 78 departures (arrivals not reported) and passenger revenues of $26.75 the same year. In 1884 the Cannon Valley (Minnesota Central) reported 355 departures and 477 arrivals, for total revenues of $100.90.

Seeing possibilities in the site, a group of men bought the mill and formed the Cascade Manufacturing Company, capitalized at $25,000. The group filed articles of incorporation with the secretary of state on April 13, 1883. The four promoters of the company were Daniel F. Akin (or Aiken) of Farmington plus David H. Orr, Ephron Lockwood, and Edwin S. Drake, all of Northfield. Orr, Lockwood and Drake, at least, took up residence at Cascade. As noted above, Lockwood apparently owned the mill in its earliest stage. These men surveyed and platted a town, half in Goodhue County and half in Dakota. Although a survey of the entire plat of 39 blocks was complete by April 7, 1883 (the northern half recorded in the Dakota County Register of Deeds office on May 18), the Goodhue County record did not appear until October 27, 1886. It shows the mill, a blacksmith shop, and a cooper shop on the south side of the river (the county line) and a grain elevator on the north.

Meanwhile, a post office had opened at Cascade, on December 28, 1882, with Arthur J. Drake postmaster. The sequence of events is not clear, but since Arthur Drake appears in an 1884 gazetteer as bookkeeper at the mill, the Drakes may already have been in business before the formation of the Cascade Manufacturing Company. A contemporary newspaper reported that after the opening of the post office, the name of the community changed from Granville to Cascade, with no reason given. On October 1, 1883, Lockwood succeeded Drake as postmaster. By 1886 (and probably two or three years earlier) he was running a general store. The post office probably operated in the store.

The village of Cascade grew rapidly and prospered for a few years. The biennial gazetteers reflect that growth, but they tend to describe towns of a year or two earlier than their dates of publication. The 1884–85 gazetteer, first to include Cascade, lists four coopers—Herman, John H., and Joseph Metz, and E. J. Austin—plus carpenter Arlin A. Scofield. Two years later, blacksmith Anton Anderson appeared on the list, along with store proprietor Lockwood and head miller Chancy Foster. Herman Metz was then operating a hotel, and an-

Pauline Anderson and blacksmith Anton Anderson of Cascade. *GCHS*

other Metz, William, was a mail carrier. By this time, however, Knut N. Myhre, formerly postmaster at Wangs, probably ran the store. Myhre replaced the postmaster at Wangs a few days before the end of 1886. Late the following year he opened a store in the new town of Dennison. The gazetteers list him as proprietor of the Cascade store as late as 1890, so he may have retained his interests there for some time.

Myhre never became postmaster at Cascade. On March 25, 1886, David H. Orr replaced Lockwood, retaining the office until its closing on March 15, 1901. Abundant contemporary references make clear that Orr gradually took over management of the Cascade mill and became virtual proprietor of the town, population 100 at the time. By 1892 he was running the store, Ervin G. Orr served as mail carrier, and B. E. Orr was "newspaper agent." The firm was now "D. H. Orr & Son." The mill was described in 1889 as a three-story building 42 by 50 feet, with a two-story wing on the east and an addition on the west.

Its capacity was 150 barrels per day. "Commodious" warehouses and cooper shops served as auxiliaries to the mill.

Although in a sense it was a company town, Cascade had an identity of its own. The center of its cultural life was the schoolhouse, which served as a church until 1889–90, when a union chapel was built. Dedicated on June 8, 1890, this chapel served as a social center as well as a house of worship. In November 1892, for example, it was the scene of a "grand entertainment" presented by the "Cascade Literary Society," one in a succession of cultural organizations briefly flourishing there. The Cascade cornet band provided the music. Several years earlier the "Cascade Dramatic & Amateur Company" had presented *The Turn of the Tide, or Wrecked in Port,* "a nautical and temperance drama in three acts" in the Randolph opera house.

Despite evidence of prosperity, Cascade's decline began as early as 1885, when the Minnesota and Northwestern Railroad Company built a north-south line just east of the village. At the point where the track crossed those built earlier, a new town named Randolph was platted that spring. Soon Randolph, better located with respect to rail transportation, overshadowed Cascade. For a time the two cooperated, at least outwardly, and even had a "Twin Cities" baseball team. But in 1889 someone proposed the erection of a new school within Randolph's boundaries to serve both communities. A meeting on July 20 saw heated discussion and defeat of the proposal by one vote. Eventually Randolph got a school of its own.

The Cascade correspondent of the *Cannon Falls Beacon* painted a rosy picture in the face of unmistakable evidence that the town was going downhill. In 1890 he wrote, "Cascade is booming if the Post Office is any criterion as it takes from three to five to distribute the mail now-a-days." Two years later he reported that two new families were moving to town. The men would work at the mill, which was running night and day. But the number of businessmen listed in the gazetteers dwindled year by year. In the 1894–95 edition, only D. H. and B. E. Orr and one blacksmith, Anderson, appeared. And in August, J. H. Metz and the manager of the Oxford mill left for Coppock, Iowa, where they had bought a mill.

The blow that killed Cascade struck suddenly. On the night of October 1–2, 1894, a fire destroyed the mill and cooper shop. The cooper shop burned first, between ten o'clock and midnight. Once it was consumed, everyone went to bed thinking there was no further danger—the building was 600 feet from the mill, and recent rains reduced the likelihood of spread. But at about 2:30 a.m. the alarm rang again. The mill was on fire and soon beyond hope of salvation. Nothing came of the rumors of intent to rebuild the next year. The 1898–99 gazetteer reported that Cascade had one of the best waterpowers in the state, with a dam in good repair but "at present not utilized." It described the site as good for a flour or woolen mill. In August 1899 a rumor floated that V. M.

Cascade, 1911, looking north up Mill Street.
Anderson's blacksmithy is in left foreground, his house to its right. *GCHS*

Walbridge had bought the Cascade site for $4,500 and was going to erect a mill there. Nothing came of this scheme, but the *Beacon* reported cryptically in 1901 "some more new prospects for a mill at Cascade"—another rumor without foundation. The days of small-scale rural milling were over, and the Cascade mill was never rebuilt. In the spring of 1903 part of the dam washed away. Anderson, the blacksmith, appeared in the 1898 listing and for some years afterward, but D. H. Orr appeared only as "farmer, real estate and loans." The store, evidently closed by 1898, was remodeled for use as a barn in 1908.

Thus by the time the post office closed, the decline of Cascade was well underway. By 1942 it was emphatically a ghost town. A reporter from the *Dakota County Tribune* of Farmington visited the site that October and interviewed Anton Anderson, who still lived there, keeping his blacksmith shop, long unused, in perfect order. The union church, standing but not in use then, was subsequently removed. Today little remains to suggest a town on the spot. Five homes, the building once housing the blacksmith shop, a few pieces of concrete along the river—those are the relics of Cascade.

The hamlet that grew around the Oxford mill, mentioned earlier, never acquired a post office. In 1867 Charles N. Wilcox, a miller for 21 years, began building a mill on the Little Cannon River, about three miles southwest of Cannon Falls. The Industrial Census of 1870 described it as a three-run mill, generating 45 horsepower. Representing an investment of $25,000, it had an annual capacity of 12,850 barrels of flour. These statistics suggest the Oxford mill was about the same-size operation as the Granville mills and substantially smaller than the Forest mills near Zumbrota.

As at Belvidere Mills and Cascade, a cluster of houses grouped about the mill gave Oxford Mills the aspect of a country village. A newspaper report in 1876 credited the community with half-a-dozen houses and a Methodist church. Two years later a school was mentioned. A more pretentious stone edifice replaced the original mill, a four-story frame structure, in 1878. With that complete, the mill owners made other improvements, including an addition of three run of stone.

On September 12, 1879, the editor of the *Cannon Falls Beacon,* Silas S. Lewis, published an account of his visit to the new mill—an example of the puffery indulged in by small-town journalism at the time:

A Model Mill

Perhaps there is not a flouring mill in the state that is so complete in all its details as is the Oxford Mills, C. N. Wilcox, proprietor, and which are situated on the Little Cannon River, about two miles from this village. We paid a visit to the mill a few days ago, viewed it from bottom to top, and we must say that we were very favorably impressed with it.

The main part of this mill was built in 1878, is constructed of stone, and is four stories in height, and is 42 feet by 54 feet, as regards size. Then, in order to facilitate matters in low water, it was found necessary to place steam fixtures into the mill. For this purpose an engine house was put up, this season, which is one story high and 32 feet by 32 feet in size. In this there has already been placed a large boiler, and an engine of 72 horse power will soon be ready to run, probably in a couple of weeks. This machinery is only to be used when the water is short.

The motive power is furnished by a 35 inch Leffel water wheel, and the power is communicated to the machinery by the means of belts, instead of gearing. The mill has four run of stone, and from the foundation to the roof is most solidly constructed, everything being placed on a stone foundation, thereby ensuring a sureness and steadiness of movement to the machinery, which is very essential in manufactories of the kind. The machinery is of the most modern and approved make and pattern.

Mr. Wilcox has spent his whole life in the flouring business, and since he commenced the erection of his present mill, he has spent a great deal of time and money in the enterprise. He now has the satisfaction of owning one of the best small mills in the state. His flour is par excellance [*sic*] and commands a ready sale in the markets. Pluck and energy are the characteristics of Mr. Wilcox and it is exemplified in all his business operations.

Although Wilcox remained proprietor of the mill for many years, the Archibald family of Dundas shared ownership from an early date. The firm was officially Archibald & Wilcox as early as 1870. In later years the local newspapers mentioned numerous changes of management, but whether these represented changes of ownership is not clear. Despite the existence of two and sometimes three mills in nearby Cannon Falls, the Oxford mill seems to have remained a profitable enterprise long after most of the county's rural mills went out of business.

As at Cascade, fire ended the career of Oxford Mills. On February 21, 1903, the mill burned, and with its destruction the hamlet lost its reason for being. In the following years recurring rumors predicted the rebuilding of the mill. A month or so after the fire, one report announced formation of a stock company to rebuild the mill, but in April the *Beacon* had to admit the plan had come to a standstill. "Unless something is done," the writer commented, "there will be very fine ruins among the beautiful scenery, and another fine water power will be going to waste."

The ruins of the Oxford mill, 1957. *RWM*

The prediction proved accurate. The Wilcox heirs tried to sell the deteriorating property in 1907 and 1908. In the latter year a flood undermined part of the stone wall. Without the mill, the community that had grown up around it gradually disappeared. The Oxford Methodist Church, built in 1873, continued in use until the late 1940s. It was torn down in the mid-1950s. The stout walls of the old stone mill are in a good state, and some have suggested a small park be established around them.

Central Point

Before Lake City developed as the leading town on Lake Pepin, Central Point, its neighbor across the line in Goodhue County, looked to an independent future. Platted on May 28, 1855, by Robert L. Phillips, Perry D. Martin, and Herman L. Barrett, the town merited an addition one year later. A post office opened there on October 22, 1855, with Perry D. Martin postmaster. Silas Cross opened a store that year, and Elias S. Harrison opened a hotel. The next year Charles W. E. Hackett built another store. For many years the town's chief industry was sawmilling. Charles N. Moe built the first steam sawmill, which apparently had a short life. Joseph Scott, Joseph W. Crawford, and C. M. Lewis built another, in 1857. Later operated by Frank Sterritt and still later by S. S. and George H. Grannis, it survived until 1892.

Central Point had a surprising number of postmasters during its short existence. Martin's successors were Charles W. Hackett starting September 18, 1856, Carter Gardner starting June 20, 1857, Charles N. Moe starting October 9, 1857, Frederick A. Johnson starting October 14, 1859, and Edwin B. Hawkins starting May 2, 1860. Presumably because the village was immediately adjacent to Lake City, the post office closed on August 7, 1860.

Central Point did not expire with its post office. In fact, its busiest days lay ahead. The Industrial Census of 1870 noted that the Grannis sawmill represented an investment of $22,000, generated 80 horsepower, and employed 22 adults and three juveniles, with an annual payroll of $4,000. In operation only four months during the previous year, it used 600,000 logs to produce lumber worth $12,800. Three years later the community built a two-story school—surely one of the largest in the county outside an incorporated city or village.

Seven years later the Central Point mill dominated the economic life of the community. The 1880 census counted the village population separately from that of the township. The population of 112 included at least a dozen people working at the sawmill. In addition to George Grannis, listed as a lumber dealer, the census included head sawyer William Coghlan, fireman George Stanton, clerk Edward Stanton, machinist Charles Frost, engineer Harrison Gill, and several young men listed as "works in sawmill." Teamster Jacob Dickey and boilermaker Willard Sevill may have been connected with the sawmill too. Central Point at that time also boasted two shoemakers, a stonemason, a milliner, and a man who "work[ed] in brickyard"—whether there or in Lake City is not known.

But almost from the beginning, Central Point's proximity to Lake City was a drag on its commercial prosperity. With the closing of the Grannis sawmill in 1892, the community drifted towards the status of a residential area for people employed in its much larger neighbor. The school continued until 1947, and the building stood for eight years after that. Until 1972 Central Point township remained politically independent. Then Lake City annexed the platted portion (and somewhat more), and the rural area became part of Florence township. Thus, after nearly 120 years, Goodhue County's smallest township ceased to exist, and the last vestige of the village's separate identity followed suit.

Claybank

Goodhue County's clay industry, centered in the northern part of Goodhue township, has been economically important since its beginnings, early in the county's history. About 1861 a German-born potter, John Paul, bought some land in what came to be called the Clay Pits, installed a potter's wheel and a kiln, and began making crocks, jugs, bowls, jars, and small statues. After about ten years he moved away, but others followed.

In 1877 the Red Wing Stoneware Company began exploiting the deposits of clay that Paul had found so valuable. Six years later Minnesota Stoneware began to compete; North Star Stoneware came on the scene in 1892. In 1906 the three merged in the Red Wing Union Stoneware Company, which changed its name in 1936 to Red Wing Pottery. The company ended its manufacture of stoneware in 1967. Meanwhile, the Red Wing Sewer Pipe Company, organized in 1891 to exploit the inferior clay discarded by the stoneware companies, continued digging after the latter firms depleted the usable deposits. In 1949 the sewer-pipe company began reworking the clay pits that had lain closed since 1925. The pits finally closed in 1972.

Upon completion of the Duluth, Red Wing & Southern Railroad Company's line in 1889, the extensive clay-digging operations, underway for nearly

Claybank store/depot, 1939. *RWM*

three decades, expanded. Partly to serve the workers in the clay pits, Henry Holst built a store just east of the railroad track in section 5, in a narrow valley broadening farther north to form the valley of Hay Creek. A post office opened with Laurits Nelson postmaster on June 30, 1890. In reply to a preliminary questionnaire from the Post Office Department, Nelson stated that the proposed office would serve 60 or 70 families. Holst succeeded Nelson as postmaster on April 22, 1892, and retained the position until August 21, 1900. Then Kurt Diercks, the new owner of the store, became postmaster. The Claybank post office closed February 29, 1904.

Claybank remained a busy place for many years. In the period of maximum activity at the clay pits, to which a branch line was built in 1892, some 75 men held jobs there. Two large boardinghouses and several family residences provided housing. Even after 1915, ticket sales at the Claybank depot amounted to $150 or $200 a month. Two grain elevators operated there for some years. In February 1914, however, the Minnesota Malting Company closed its elevator. A farmers' shipping association formed to take it over later that year. The Claybank Farmers' Grain Company, organized August 5, 1921, with capitalization of $10,000 divided into 1,000 shares, succeeded that firm, buying a grain house from the Fleischmann Malting Company and selling the old elevator for $252. It was torn down, and in time this firm also closed.

Sold to William and Henry Santelman in 1904, the Claybank store prospered. The community seemed to have prospects even after it lost its post office. In 1907 four new houses went up, and the Claybank correspondent of the *Goodhue Enterprise* predicted that "in population and importance Claybank will soon be a close second to Goodhue." Nothing of the sort occurred, but the store remained in business many years. In 1915 it passed to Edmund Berg, who operated it until 1947. Elmer Bremer then ran it for a year and a half, before selling out to Clara Lostetter and her son Harold.

After activity at the clay pits dwindled, the store depended on farmer patronage, which it solicited through a delivery system. During Berg's long tenure as owner, he converted the delivery from horse-drawn wagon to motor truck. The service picked up eggs and delivered groceries within a six-mile radius. This device was not enough to save the Claybank store from the effects of rapid transportation and competition from larger towns. On August 28 and 29, 1958, the store held an auction of the stock and furnishings, after which the store part of the building was converted to residential use. (Berg had built an addition to the store for a dwelling.) Since the depot, a remodeled boxcar, had been removed some years earlier, the closing of the store brought to an end the 69-year history of the Claybank community. The building was subsequently razed. With the abandonment of the rail line in 1965 and removal of the track the following year, little is left to suggest the once-busy trading center at Claybank.

Crystal Springs

Among the early post offices of little record is Crystal Springs, established on July 2, 1858, and discontinued on December 3, 1863. The only postmaster during its short life was George Gay, a native of Massachusetts who had come to Minnesota, after a brief stop in Iowa, when the area opened to settlement. He located in Belvidere township. According to the 1860 census, which gave his age as 32, he owned real estate valued at $7,500, making him one of the leading farmers in the township. He was elected to the post of constable in 1859, when the original 72-square-mile township divided, with the western half organized as Lime (later Goodhue).

The Sewall map shows a *Mineral* Springs (evidently an error for *Crystal* Springs) in the southern part of Belvidere, in the southwest quarter of section 27. An 1894 county atlas shows a "Crystal Springs Farm" and locates the springs in the northeast part of section 34. The short-lived post office probably was somewhere in this vicinity.

Eagle Mills

Of all the post offices in Goodhue County, none left slighter trace in contemporary records than Eagle Mills. Established on May 14, 1860, with Warren Mills postmaster, it closed just 18 months later, on November 14, 1861. Though the *Goodhue County Republican* (Red Wing) noted its establishment, no indi-

In 1878, W. S. Lowery built a flour mill at the village of Eagle Mills.
In 1886 the village changed its name to Welch. *GCHS*

cation of its location appeared. Since the name Eagle Mills applied to the locality where Welch village later arose, the Eagle Mills post office probably lived
its brief existence there. The 1886 application for the Welch post office carried
the dateline Eagle Mills.

Its only postmaster also had a short life. The census of 1860, taken in June,
listed a W. Mills, age 29, carpenter, living in Red Wing. The listing of his place
of birth is illegible, but his wife, Lydia, was a native of New Hampshire. They
had a daughter, Ida, age nine months. Mills owned real estate worth $800 and
a personal estate valued at $550. The *Goodhue County Republican* for August
8, 1862, reported the death of Warren Mills, age 31, and his daughter, Ida, 2½,
both of diphtheria. We know little of this man, even less of the post office over
which he presided for 18 months.

The name Eagle Mills continued in use until the name Welch supplanted
it in 1886. The mill, built by the firm of Miller and Lowery, had a history
of misfortune. In the summer of 1880 the dam washed out. That fall Miller
died in a railroad accident in Red Wing. The following spring W. S. Lowery,
thrown from his wagon while on his way to Red Wing, also died. In the summer of 1885, someone from Minneapolis (possibly Prentiss Clark, proprietor of the second Belle Creek) bought the mill after a period of inactivity
and put it in running order. In 1886, a store opened nearby, and the Welch post
office was established.

Eggleston
The northernmost post office in Goodhue County was Eggleston, established
December 27, 1875, on the line of the Chicago, Milwaukee & St. Paul, built
five years earlier. The village of Eggleston grew up on the border between
Welch and Burnside townships, and the post office operated in one or the other,
depending on the location of the building currently housing it. Its name honored John E. and Joseph Eggleston, who settled in 1855 in the area later divided
between Welch and Burnside. The first postmaster, Franklin M. Allen, served
until October 27, 1879, when Reinholdt Peterson, who ran a store for a while,
succeeded him. Michael T. Nilan replaced Peterson on March 30, 1882, inau-
gurating more than half a century of Nilan family postmastership.

Born in Pittsburgh, Michael Nilan came to Eggleston in the early 1880s to
take charge of a grain elevator and operate a small store there. In 1902 he built
a larger store. He also served many years as station agent. As a trading center
Eggleston mainly served the area known as Prairie Island. When that section
of the county lost population, the village economy suffered. The biennial gazetteers do not reveal much of a town there at any time, though the one for 1882–
83 mentions a second store, run by J. Rosby & Bros. Farmers of the area organized a cooperative creamery capitalized at $25,000 on May 1, 1920, but its
career was brief. Except for the Nilan store, which burned in 1930, whatever

The Nilan store at Eggleston. *GCHS*

other businesses Eggleston may have boasted closed their doors. A 1922 gazetteer listed only the store, a fur-and-hide business run by E. P. Nilan, and the creamery. Four years later a radio shop appeared, and the Eggleston Creamery and Produce Company had become the Vermillion Creamery Company. The grain elevator, though long unused, was not torn down until 1947.

Because of the comparative remoteness of the Prairie Island locality, the Eggleston post office remained in operation many years. Edward P. Nilan became postmaster on May 20, 1918, followed on November 25, 1921, by Helen M. Nilan, in turn replaced by Michael T. Nilan Jr., on May 22, 1924. After a short period beginning November 10, 1925, when Martin G. Nilan served, M. T. Nilan Jr. returned to the position January 31, 1927, retaining the office until it closed on August 31, 1934. A rural route from Welch then was extended to serve Prairie Island and the Eggleston vicinity.

After the creamery went out of business, Leo Kinney rented the building in 1937 for use as a general store. In 1947, Kinney built a new store, transforming the old creamery into a pony barn. It was later razed. The Eggleston store continued to serve as a trading point for the Prairie Island population, including the Indian community there, and for fishermen and hunters who frequented the sloughs along the Mississippi. It was a popular place for fish fries and wedding dances. After Leo Kinney died in 1962, his wife, Val, continued to run the store until 1979. In 1982 Colleen Kinney and her sister Georgene opened a restaurant in the building, also carrying a small stock of groceries. This business closed in 1985. The Kinney store building still stands, transformed into a residence and the office for a trailer court that gives Eggleston a larger population than it ever had in its heyday.

Eggleston, which started as a railroad station, no longer has a railway. To accommodate growing traffic, the Milwaukee built a track across Prairie Island for westbound trains in 1909. In 1941 the railroad company, switching to double-track, abandoned the original track there. Rails were taken up the following year, the depot demolished in 1946.

Eidsvold

The Norwegian settlement of the 1850s, which has given western Goodhue County its distinctive character, began in Wanamingo and Holden townships. From a center near the post office of Norway, it radiated in all directions—to Warsaw, Leon, Minneola, Kenyon, Cherry Grove, and Roscoe townships. As we have seen, Norwegian names appeared early among the postmasters of offices such as Ayr. In some instances, post offices opened in all-Norwegian communities with names reminiscent of places in the Old Country. One of these was Eidsvold, in the southern part of section 23 and the northern part of section 26, Holden township, less than two-and-a-half miles from Norway. This post office opened July 26, 1875, with Hans Christensen postmaster. Christensen, whose name also appears as Christianson and Hans Christianson Westermo, seems to have operated a blacksmith shop at Eidsvold, which, according to an 1877 map, also contained a schoolhouse and a second blacksmith shop.[4] The *Minnesota State Gazetteer* for 1878–79 also lists a general store—"Forening Dovre Handels." Dovre, like Eidsvold, is a Norwegian place name, the birthplace of some local settlers. Long after the post office and hamlet of Eidsvold disappeared, the rural school continued as the Dovre school. The Eidsvold post office closed June 29, 1888, and the government property, as well as all the mail, went to the Norway post office.

Elmira

One of the more important early roads over which mail traveled was that from Red Wing to Zumbrota and points south. Laid out before the townships were formally organized, this road roughly followed the present route of T.H. 58 to a point near the north line of what is now Goodhue township. From there it followed the present route of Goodhue County Highway 4 to section 23, then continued in a southwesterly direction to cross the boundary into Zumbrota township about where Highway 58 now crosses the town line. Because of the traffic on this road, two of the earliest settlers of Goodhue township, John Mann and David Hickok, opened their homes to the public as hotels in 1855.

In February 1857 part of the northeast quarter of section 11 was surveyed and platted as the town of Elmira. The plat recorded on July 14, 1857, covered an area of 58.2 acres and contained 16 numbered and four lettered blocks, including one labeled "Public Grounds" and another divided into a "Church Lot" and a "School Lot." Among the ten named streets were the usual Washington and Franklin, as well as one for Hickok.[5] The proprietor of the town was Cyrus Crouch, later to serve on the first township board of supervisors.

Besides laying out a paper city, the promoters of Elmira established a post office on April 29, 1857, with David Hickok (or Hickox) postmaster. He served only until June 1, when Cyrus Crouch took over. On April 5, 1858, the name of the office was changed to Goodhue Centre, with Peter Easterly its postmaster. Easterly arrived on the scene in 1856 and, discovering more business than Mann and Hickok could handle, opened a third hotel, on the northwest quarter of section 23. This became the site of the Goodhue Centre post office.

The name Elmira did not vanish immediately. Upon organization of the townships in 1858, the present Goodhue township was, with Belvidere, part of a larger township called York. When the committee for designating townships learned on August 23, 1858, that the name York was in use elsewhere in the state, it offered the name Elmira—on September 15. With this also rejected, in December, another committee proposed the name Belvidere. Elmira survived even this blow and appears on the Sewall map as the only place named between Red Wing and Zumbrota. The name continued on delinquent tax lists published in newspapers as late as 1864, but the plat must have been vacated shortly afterward. As with Troy, no record of its vacation is available. The proprietors of some of these paper cities probably did not go through the legal formalities necessary for platting townsites. Hence some sites were vacated by default rather than by legal action.

Fair Point
The treatment by each of the five histories of the ghost town of Fair Point well illustrates the tendency of county historians to rely on their predecessors. Mitchell's 1869 history notes that Thomas Haggard and a Mr. Beckwith laid out a village plat in 1857. It also states that a post office established in 1858, with Silas Merriam postmaster, closed in 1861. Two years later, it continues, the first buildings went up, and in 1866 the post office reopened, with Herman Eastman postmaster. This story, repeated with slight variation in every subsequent history, is inaccurate in several details. The post office opened on October 23, 1857 (not 1858), and David M. Haggard (not Merriam) was the first postmaster. Merriam replaced Haggard on May 23, 1860. The post office closed July 20, 1861. Upon reestablishment of the office on March 2, 1865 (not 1866), Alvin D. Williams was postmaster. Eastman followed him on January 18, 1867. David Haggard (not Thomas) made a claim in July 1857 to part of the land later occupied by the village, in section 33 of Cherry Grove. Truman Beckwith the same year filed a claim in the next section. A plat of Fair Point may have been surveyed as Mitchell said, but no record of it exists in the county recorder's office today. Some later newspapers refer perhaps facetiously to named streets, but there is no other hint of a plat.

Whatever the truth of its founding, Fair Point was for many years a thriving crossroads village and trading point. If some of its early postmasters are but shadows, the later ones emerge more clearly. The Haggards—Thomas and David—were early settlers who took up land claims in the Fair Point area in 1856 and 1857. The former, age 42 in 1860, was born in Kentucky and had moved to Iowa, where two of his children were born. Of Merriam and Williams less is known. Eastman's name, however, appears in print often enough to be identifiable. According to the 1869 history, he and E. B. Jewitt opened a store at Fair Point in 1867. Jewitt seems not to have remained with the firm long, for an 1872 gazetteer lists Eastman & Russell as the store's proprietors. An "E. [Elisha] Russell, gen. store" is also on the list. This may be a duplication, but with the post office changing hands that year, Eastman may have withdrawn, leaving the business to Russell.

Eastman's successor as postmaster was Joseph H. Kelsey, appointed April 1, 1872. Kelsey, then about 27, had come to Goodhue County in 1855 with his parents, Wilson and Lucinda (Brooks) Kelsey, from New York State, with a pause in Wisconsin. He opened a store at Fair Point in 1870. By 1878 the firm of J. H. Kelsey & Bro. (Byron) had the only store in the village, which by that time boasted blacksmiths V. W. Sterling and A. W. Taft, photographer Alfred Morell, horseshoer E. Russell, wagonmaker E. Garrison, pump manufacturer M. G. Scofield, a hotel run by the postmaster's father Wilson Kelsey, and two churches—German Lutheran (erected in 1865) and Wesleyan Methodist. The post office then served 200 people, but most of the patrons and probably some of the businesses lived or operated outside the immediate Fair Point community. In 1880, when the Census Bureau provided figures for several unincorporated places in the county, it credited Fair Point with 60 inhabitants. Among the 13 family heads were five farmers, one farm laborer, one blacksmith, one storekeeper, one store clerk, one stonemason, one wagonmaker, one harnessmaker, and one physician.

According to the gazetteers, the business life of Fair Point endured a chronic high rate of turnover. An 1880 issue listed only J. H. Kelsey, Garrison, and Sterling of those included two years earlier. Added were express and railroad agent A. A. Merchant, (there was no railroad then or ever in Fair Point), physician C. P. Gibson, and shoemaker J. K. Wyman. Two years later Kelsey, Garrison, and Wyman appeared again, plus harnessmakers Blackmer & Billings, blacksmith Charles Rathkey, grocer U. V. Russell, and meat marketer B. Stockwell. By 1884 J. H. Kelsey was running the hotel as well as a store (the Russell store burned in 1883). The firm of Kelsey and Charlton started a creamery the previous year in response to the wishes of local farmers. Standbys Garrison and Wyman were still in business. Harnessmaker Edward Blasdell and blacksmith Charles Hinkle augmented the village's commercial activity as well.

Kelsey's various involvements apparently left him no time to be postmaster. Still listed as storekeeper, hotel proprietor, and part owner of the creamery in 1886, he gave up the position to Christopher R. Drew on May 14, 1884. Except for a period of ill health—March 10, 1874, to April 13, 1875, when William C. Kelsey acted in his stead—Joseph Kelsey held the position for more than 12 years, longer than any other holder of the office there. On March 17, 1886, John Wunderlich became postmaster. Bernard Devlin followed on August 22, 1888. Adam Jahn succeeded Devlin on March 22, 1890.

The rapid changes in postmaster reflect the frequent turnover of local businesses, suggesting a decline in economic prosperity. Late in 1886 a wagonmaker moved his shop to Roscoe. Despite denials then that Martin Wunderlich & Son would sell the store, it did so the next March. In 1888 a gazetteer gave Fair Point 41 inhabitants, listing only the creamery, the two blacksmiths (Hinkle and John Hoff), and the two churches. John Wunderlich was still postmaster, but there is no mention of a store. Hoff (or Hauff) left the village in the spring of 1890; there was not enough business for two blacksmiths. The status of the creamery seems to have changed as well, for in October 1888 Charles Sherwood and a man named Bols started a cheese factory, apparently in the former creamery building. Although this factory got off to a good start, by March of 1891 Sherwood was selling his vats and presses to go out of business. This did not mark the end of the dairy industry at Fair Point. Almost at once there was agitation for a successor to the cheese factory. By the middle of May, Marvin & Cammack, of the Crescent Creamery Company of Faribault, had started a creamery at Fair Point, as well as at other points in the region.

Other Fair Point businesses found survival difficult, but there were always people willing to try. For a short time the village had two stores. Adam Jahn and his brother Henry, who succeeded him as postmaster on April 1, 1892, participated in several enterprises in the village, including a general store that ran from 1890 or earlier to 1896. About the beginning of 1891 Cortland D. Hunt (once Ayr's postmaster) opened a second store, and a newspaper item described Fair Point as "a good place to trade." But in October of the same year it reported that Hunt had sold out to his brother, S. A. Hunt, who was to remove the stock. In 1892 a gazetteer credited Fair Point with a store run by Mrs. M. John [Jahn], a hotel run by Mrs. [Ida] J. F. Russell, blacksmith Hinkle, and "A. Jahn, painter."

Henry Jahn was said in October 1892 to have resigned his position as postmaster, but he was still on the job the next August, replying to complaints by the *Kenyon Leader's* Cherry Grove correspondent that mail service at Fair Point was irregular. On September 12, 1893, however, Ancil (Ansel) Vanderwalker, who apparently had opened a store, took the position. His is the only store mentioned in an 1896 gazetteer. Hinkle was still the village blacksmith at that time, Jacob Stussy was running a stage service, John Williams was a carpenter, and A. Jahn and Henry Jahn appeared as painter and "manufacturer's agent" respectively. In addition, A. J. Hunt was "advertising agent." In February 1896 the *Leader* correspondent reported that "our store is in shape to do business and we are glad to say that they are doing some." Whose store it was is not clear, though probably it was Vanderwalker's. The phrasing of the item suggests the business was less than booming. A few months later Earl Dickey, who earlier had run a store at Forest Mills, opened another in the building formerly occupied by Henry Jahn. Never mentioned in the biennial gazetteers, this enterprise did not last long, for by 1899 Dickey worked in Minneapolis.

If commercial activity of the conventional sort was declining at Fair Point in the 1890s, another enterprise was flourishing. This was a matrimonial agency, run mainly by Henry Jahn with assistance from Earl Hunt and others. A five-page publication listed people seeking mates. Some of the county newspaper "unmercifully roasted" the concern, which was ready to give anyone "a lift on the road to matrimonial bliss." The *Red Wing Daily Republican* began:

> At one of the smaller post offices in this county some genius is operating a concern which bears the imposing title of the National Matrimonial Agency, and he is industriously employed in sending out by mail what purport to be lists of women in search of male correspondents.

The article continues in the vein of righteous indignation mingled with amusement, implying that the agency was a simple fraud. Despite such ridicule, business was good enough several months later for Jahn to talk of buying a cylinder press. But in the spring of 1896 the agency moved to Cannon City, in Rice County, where "Cupid's Column" continued to serve its clientele. Henry's brother Peter had bought a store there, and a sister, Elizabeth, became postmaster at Dean (the post office name of Cannon City) on May 18, 1896. Henry followed late in June with his press and other equipment.

Earlier, Fair Point had supported a periodical of a more general nature. In November 1889 the *Fairpoint Illuminator,* a "spicy little sheet," made its appearance. Henry Haggard was editor and a Miss Russell his assistant. The many but little-detailed references to this publication do not reveal anything about its format or means of reproduction and not much about its contents. It seems to have been a gossip sheet, distributed (or perhaps only read aloud) at "sociables," as was the case late in 1890, when George Callister was editor. Whatever the *Illuminator* was, its existence suggests a degree of community identity that vanished from rural areas within a few decades.

The Fairpoint (the spelling changed in 1895) post office went to Cortland D. Hunt, on January 13, 1899. But he declined the job, and Henry E. Fairbank took it on March 3. Fairbank held the position only until June 14, when Joseph Henry succeeded him. By this time business seems largely to have petered out

Fairpoint School #97, 1952. *RWM*

at Fairpoint village. The post office moved to Henry's farm in section 28, more than a mile from its former site. Vanderwalker's store but no other Fairpoint business appeared in a 1900 gazetteer, which gave Fairpoint only 25 residents. With the coming of RFD, the post office closed, on January 31, 1902.

Fairpoint did not utterly disappear. A creamery or cheese factory of some kind continued in business there, under various auspices, for many years. Early in the 20th century Godfrey Andrist operated a factory there. In 1912 he sold his plant and a quarter acre of land to the newly organized Fairpoint Cooperative Cheese Association for $1,200. Since this tract of land is essentially the same shown on an 1894 map as belonging to Charles A. Sherwood, the building probably is the one that was used for the manufacture of cheese from 1888 to 1891. Organized March 26, 1912, the Fairpoint cooperative renewed its corporate existence in 1932 and continued making cheese until 1946. Then, like most of the other rural cheese factories and creameries of the region, it finally succumbed. In about 1924 Kenneth Zeller took the job of cheesemaker. Still in his teens and for several years the youngest cheesemaker in the state, he gave the Fairpoint factory a reputation for excellence. In 1926 the co-op did $26,277.43 worth of business. The next year cheese from the factory won first prize in the state contest with an average score of 99.91 percent, reportedly the best record of any factory in Minnesota or Wisconsin. Though all the other business places had long since vanished, a gasoline pump operated in conjunction with the cheese factory in its later years.

When the cheese factory closed, Goodhue County Cooperative Electric cut service to the building on March 24, 1946, and Fairpoint village ceased to be. A German Evangelical church that long stood west of the factory eventually closed. In the early 1930s it was moved a half-mile south, to serve many more years as a community hall. Today this building and the nearby rural school (still in use in 1954) are gone. The shell of the cheese factory, bleak and lonely on its hill for several years, was torn down late in 1963. A new house, the foundations of two recently razed houses, and the Evangelical cemetery comprise Fairpoint today.

Featherstone
One of the first settlers in Featherstone township was Asahel D. Roberts, a native of New York, who in January 1856 took up a claim in the southwest quarter of section 21. On October 23, 1858, he became postmaster at a new post office named for the township and presumably located on Roberts's farm, about a mile northeast of the site of the later Burley post office and not far from the present Featherstone township hall. Since Roberts retained the office until its closing on September 29, 1863, it probably was not moved during its five-year life. Featherstone appears on the Sewall map.

Finney
In August 1882 the *Red Wing Argus* reported that a new post office had opened in Goodhue County, in the township of the same name, along the Red Wing-to-Zumbrota road. (This is not the road mentioned in connection with the Elmira post office. Rather, it is the route now followed by Goodhue County Highway 6, which passes a mile west of Goodhue village.) Known as Finney because of its proximity to Jonathan Finney's place, the new post office, established July 31, was in the charge of Gustaf O. Miller. At age 18 Miller had begun farming on the east half of the northwest quarter of section 29, Goodhue township. Then he opened a general store in his house across the road from the Finney place. With no nearby post office, he persuaded the Post Office Department of the need for one at his store.

The Finney post office closed February 26, 1883, less than seven months after its establishment. Mail for its patrons went to White Willow. That spring Miller moved to White Rock, where he started or helped start a store, a telephone company, a creamery, and a bank.

Florence
Besides the principal town of Frontenac, Florence township once boasted a second village, named for the township and located along the lake in section 24. With survey done in 1857, proprietors Calvin Potter, Joseph D. Spinney, and James Sutherland recorded the plat, complete with streets and blocks, on Au-

gust 18 the next year. Most of the streets never came to be. Potter became the first postmaster of the Florence office on June 30, 1858. Aaron G. Hudson followed on July 11, 1861. Together, these men held the position for seven of its slightly more than nine years. Three others served in the remainder: M. C. Johnston from June 29, 1865; D. B. Anderson from November 6, 1865; and Milton Young from March 26, 1866. The office closed October 14, 1867.

Florence village outlived its post office by several years. The 1880 census credited it with 46 inhabitants—all farmers or farm laborers and their families. The plat was vacated in two installments—in 1886 and 1929—but delinquent tax lists referred to lots in the "former town of Florence" as late as the 1960s.

Forest Mills

As mentioned earlier, four of the discontinued post offices in the county owed their existence to milling enterprises giving rise to villages. Of these four communities, the one most completely dependent on milling was Forest Mills, on the Zumbro River about two miles east of Zumbrota.

Forest Mills existed as a town for more than ten years before it acquired a post office. In the spring of 1867, H. H. Palmer, a Zumbrota storekeeper, and William S. Wells, a Civil War veteran with landholdings in the vicinity, began construction of a four-run flour mill. Associated with them in the early years of the mill was William Bruce Dickey, also a veteran, whose connection with the town extended over a longer period than that of the other two men. Palmer withdrew from the firm soon after the mill commenced operation in 1868. Two

The mill foundation at Forest Mills, 1941. *RWM*

Red Wing grain merchants, later governor Lucius F. Hubbard and W. P. Brown, took his place. For a decade, the mill ran under the name Hubbard, Wells & Company. Wells and Dickey ran it alone for a brief period, then with others formed the Forest Mills Company in 1879, retaining principal ownership.

The mill proprietors early added several auxiliary enterprises, including a cooper shop, a warehouse, and a general store. The growing community gained a blacksmith shop, two livery barns, a sash-and-door factory, a harness shop, boardinghouses, and other businesses directly or indirectly dependent on the mill. By 1871 the mill had added a fifth run of stone, making it one of the largest country mills in the county. Before this addition, the amount invested in the mill was $50,000. According to the Industrial Census of 1870 it had an annual output of $85,000 in flour (24,500 barrels), $12,000 in feed, and $13,000 worth of barrels. The population then included four millers, four coopers, and two teamsters. At first the company provided houses for its employees. Later it sold lots to those who wished to build their own homes. As early as 1870 a village had begun to grow around the mill, and the passing decade witnessed its further development.

During these years the milling company hauled flour to Red Wing by team and shipped it down the Mississippi River, eventually to points on the East Coast or Europe. The need for a more direct access to these markets led the milling company to become interested in a railroad. It acquired a controlling interest in Minnesota Midland Railroad, which in 1877–78 built a narrow-gauge line up the Zumbro River from Wabasha to Zumbrota. During the year that brought the railroad to Forest Mills, the town was formally platted, not on the ambitious scale of the earlier "paper cities" but in conformity with its development during the previous decade. There were only eight streets: Main Street in the valley, High Street on the bluffs above, and six connecting streets running up the slopes.

Until this time Forest Mills, though it must have had at least 100 inhabitants (the census of 1880 gave it 124), had obtained its mail from the Zumbrota post office. On January 3, 1879, a post office opened in Forest Mills with Dickey as postmaster, Apparently he kept it in the store. Then, on August 22, 1884, Nels M. Olson became postmaster, keeping it for a time in his house and later in an upstairs room in the mill, where he was grain buyer.

The reason for this change was a disastrous turn of events for the milling company. Because of changes in raising wheat and in the milling industry, plus its heavy investment in Minnesota Midland, the Forest Mills Company was declared insolvent on June 21, 1884. For 18 months the mill was closed, and its employees sought work elsewhere. Then the mill was sold at auction for a fraction of its original cost (including expensive improvements). The Rust Milling Company—John R. Rust, of St. Johnsbury, Vermont, proprietor—reopened the mill late in 1885. It ran with apparent success until the summer of

1887, when it again closed. Later that year it reopened under the name Rust & Mason. The proprietors—Rust and his head miller, J. R. Mason—operated the mill for ten years more with modest and gradually declining profits, as the general economic conditions leading to the mill's original failure became more painfully acute. Meanwhile, the post office changed hands and location. On May 23, 1888, Mrs. Ellen M. Sones, station agent at the Forest Mills depot, became postmaster, and the office was moved to the depot. Effie M. Murphy succeeded her in both capacities three years later, on May 25, 1891, and retained the office until it closed.

The 1890s were years of decay for Forest Mills. Although Dickey, who remained in the village after the failure of the Forest Mills Company, ran a creamery during most of this decade, other businesses one by one closed their doors. The store closed down in 1896, when Earl C. Dickey, the proprietor, moved his stock to Fair Point. Most of the other businesses were gone by then. The end came in 1898 when Rust withdrew from the milling company, and a new firm—Mason, Olson & Engelhart—formed. It promptly dismantled the mill and reerected it at Mazeppa, where Engelhart lived. Though the feed mill and elevator remained at Forest Mills another 15 or 16 years, it was not enough to keep the village alive. The post office closed down on August 25, 1898, about the same time as the railroad station.

When the narrow-gauge line reached Faribault in 1903, some looked to a Forest Mills revival. Theodore Stecher of Zumbrota bought the mill property intending to use its waterpower to operate a tannery. Nothing came of this scheme, but Stecher put in a cement dam in 1907 and continued to run the feed mill until about 1914. In 1912 local farmers organized a cooperative and erected a small cheese factory, but the enterprise lasted only two years.

With the feed mill and elevator dismantled in 1917 and 1918, not much remained at Forest Mills. The houses that had sheltered 124 in 1880 gradually fell to the crane or mover, until only seven occupied dwellings remained. The frame cheese factory stood for many years, slowly crumbling from neglect. It was razed in 1943, its lumber used for a private garage. The Forest Mills school, built in 1871, closed its doors in 1945. The consolidated district later sold it. The building of six new houses since 1948 has not materially changed the general picture of slow decay that characterized Forest Mills after removal of the mill. Nothing about the sleepy hamlet of today recalls the excitement centering on the mill more than 120 years ago.

Goodhue Centre

Successor to the old Elmira post office and predecessor to the present Goodhue post office, Goodhue Centre had a checkered career. Closed four times, it reopened as many, though not always at the same site. It first opened April 5, 1858, when the name Elmira became Goodhue Centre, with Peter Easterly postmaster. Easterly's hotel had a considerable local reputation. The *Red Wing Sentinel* in 1860 mentioned "a humble log cabin" on the route to Oronoco and commented on its excellent food and genuine hospitality. "The man that 'can't keep a hotel,'" remarked the writer, "can learn how by calling on Easterly." Incidentally, the name of the post office refers to the county, not the township, which did not separate from Belvidere until 1859 or acquire the name Goodhue until January 1860.

Although it closed on October 23, 1860, the Goodhue Centre post office reopened December 1 of the same year, with Helen Easterly postmaster, presumably at the same site, on section 23. Closed again August 22, 1863, it reopened April 12, 1864, with John V. H. Bailey postmaster. Bailey's place was in section 11, a couple of miles north of the Easterly hotel but still along the old Red Wing-Zumbrota road, at or near the site of the earlier Elmira post office. John Gleason, who also lived in section 11, a half-mile south of the Bailey place, replaced him on December 10, 1866. Gerhard Gatz, an immigrant from Holland, operated a blacksmith shop in the vicinity around 1870. For more than 12 years, Gleason held the post office, which on June 17, 1879, went back to Bailey. The following October 27 it closed because, according to the *Red Wing Argus*, no one wanted the job.

After nearly three years, the post office reopened on July 17, 1882, under the name Goodhue, with Frank Drurig (or Durig) postmaster. A county history pinpoints its location at the old Easterly place, near which a man named Mutz ran a blacksmith shop. On December 8, 1884, the office again closed, its patrons instructed to get their mail at Hay Creek. More than three years elapsed before the office was reestablished as Goodhue Centre, on May 1, 1888. George Uslar, who was running a general store then, was postmaster. The site was the same as that under Drurig, in section 23.

When the Duluth, Red Wing & Southern Railroad built its line from Red Wing to Zumbrota in 1889, it also built a station on section 21 in Goodhue township. Soon a village developed there. Since this was the logical place for the post office, the Goodhue Centre office moved there on September 21, 1889, its name now Goodhue. Since Uslar had the previous June "made an assignment for the benefit of his creditors," the general store probably closed down about the same time.

At no time did Goodhue Centre become the nucleus of a town or even much of a rural trade center. It was just a country post office serving farm families. In the early days, at least, its business was extremely small. David Hancock, who carried the mail on several routes in the 1850s, later told a county historian that one of his duties was to collect the revenue due the government from each office on his route. His first collection at Goodhue Centre, representing the government's share of the business for the previous three months, was six cents.

Hader

In no other Goodhue County "ghost town" is the disparity between intention and achievement more evident than in Hader. Platted on an ambitious scale and intended as the county seat, it failed to fulfill the hopes of its founders. But it did become a way station on the St. Paul-Dubuque road and later an important trading point in a productive farming area. Only its failure to attract a railroad prevented Hader from becoming a principal village of the county. Today it is only a hamlet, with two former stores used as dwellings, a defunct cheese factory serving as a repair shop, and five or six houses.

When the stage line changed its route so as to follow approximately the present route of U.S. 52 between Cannon Falls and Zumbrota, the point at which the Red Wing-Kenyon road crossed it became the natural location for a town. Thus Hader came into being in 1857. On April 17 of that year a post office opened with Joshua C. Pierce postmaster. The office closed December 19 but reopened nine days later, with Pierce again postmaster. Samuel T. Babbitt replaced him on January 15, 1858, lasting only until April 12. Shubael Wales followed. Wales, who made a claim on the future site of Hader in June 1856, is the only one of the three for whom more than a name survives. Born in Vermont in 1818, he migrated to Massachusetts, then to Minnesota.

Meanwhile, the townsite of Hader was platted in June of 1857 and recorded on August 22 that year. Occupying all of section 1 of Wanamingo township (except the extreme southwest corner) and a small part of section 12, the plat was 122 blocks in size. One block was reserved for the county court house. The proprietor was Otis F. Smith, another name saved from oblivion by a thread. Although the streets were never laid out, neither was any part of the plat vacated until Sivert O. Haugen, who owned much of the eastern half of section 1, did so with his portion in 1940.

Hader had an extraordinarily high rate of turnover among its postmasters during its early years. After serving nearly four years, Wales gave way on March 17, 1862, to Thomas W. Hanson, followed on August 22, 1863, by Joseph T. Leet. On January 18, 1867, Wales returned to hold the office nearly two years. On December 16, 1868, John W. Jameson became postmaster, followed on March 4, 1870, by Samuel Arnold. A prosperous farmer and native of New York, Andrew P. Jackson held the position briefly in 1871, from April 10, when he was appointed, until June 2, when Arnold came back. Except for the sketchy information provided by the decennial census schedules, nothing is known of these men. The town is almost as obscure, but it was the scene of the county fair in 1870. An 1872 gazetteer listed a general store operated by D. Collins, as well as two blacksmiths, a shoemaker, and a cabinet maker. It made no mention of Hans P. Olson, who had appeared in the 1870 census as a "watch tinker." Thomas T. Cochran was running the store by 1873, and he became postmaster on June 28. His tenure in the office was as brief as those of his predecessors, for on March 31, 1875, Gustaff A. Ryden (several spellings) replaced him.

Ryden's appointment documents the replacement by Scandinavians of the settlers who started the town. All succeeding postmasters bore Norwegian names. The names listed in an 1878 gazetteer reflected that change. Besides William H. Purdy (1828–1895), who then ran a hotel, these others ran businesses in Hader: John Ryden (who became postmaster April 10, 1876), P. E. Dahl, and H. O. Jaishow (perhaps a printer's error), who operated stores. B. Halvorson was a carpenter. Thomas P. Storseth was a shoemaker. J. L. Goxal and Hans Harrison were blacksmiths. Christian Hveem, late of Aspelund, was now practicing medicine at Hader. The place supposedly had 60 inhabitants.

The Hader correspondent for the *Cannon Falls Beacon* remarked in July 1878: "From the silence which reigns at this place one would be led to think that Hader was a place of the past, and not the bright business center which the visitor will find who may give us a call." What he meant by silence is unclear, but he went on to say that business was brisk at all three stores and the "City Hotel" had been remodeled so to be hardly recognizable.

Two years later, when a gazetteer credited Hader with 75 residents, only one store, operated by the firm of Rosvold and Holstad, remained. Andrew Rosvold and Hans O. Holstad were immigrants from Norway, then in their early twenties. Rosvold had been in business at Hader as early as the summer of 1878. On March 8, 1879, three days after he became postmaster, Rosvold entered into a partnership with Holstad. In the preceding 22 years, 11 men served as postmaster; in the remaining 24 years four men held the job. The Rosvold-Holstad partnership dissolved in 1882; on May 14, 1883, Holstad became postmaster. Business changes were fewer in Hader during this period than in many hamlets of similar size. Blacksmiths came and went, but gazetteers continued to list much the same names year after year. By 1884, when the village reportedly had 100 residents, H. M. Hjermstad ran a feed mill there. A lawyer, P. S. Aslakson, also gave Hader as his address. In 1889 Purdy left Hader and rented the hotel to C. Thompson. E. Sweatland ran it three years later, after Purdy had sold his farm and hotel to O. S. Haugen, father of Sivert O. Haugen.

In 1894 Holstad sold his store to the firm of Larson & Ohnstad, and on July 21 Joseph O. Ohnstad (or Onstad) became postmaster. At least one other store seems to have operated during most or all of this time, under various management. In April 1894 the Hader correspondent for the *Zumbrota News* reported that Hader was "booming." Although such claims warrant skepticism, there seems to have been a good deal of business activity in Hader during the mid-1890s. Daniel Lindsay was proprietor of a general store in 1896, when Hader also had two millinery shops. Early the next year the Zumbrota firm of Erstad, Haugen & Company reportedly was building a new store east of Larson & Ohnstad's. A store erected by Olaus Larson in "North Hader" in the 1870s was in operation off and on until its conversion to a church in 1897. The Rev. K. O.

Lundeberg and others conducted evangelistic services at the "Nazareth" church until about 1915. It was torn down in 1918.

Hader's last postmaster was Ole T. Teigen, appointed February 27, 1899. A month earlier Teigen had replaced Ohnstad of the firm Larson & Ohnstad in ownership of the store. In 1900 Hader, credited with a population 65, contained three blacksmiths (one of whom doubled as a shoemaker), a furniture dealer, and a hotel run by S. O. (Sivert) Haugen, in addition to the Larson and Teigen store. Two years later, Edward Haller, who had formerly owned the store in "North Hader," became Teigen's partner, keeping the store in business until his death in 1908. He ran it alone during the last two years.

The Hader post office, another casualty of RFD, came to an end in 1903, the year of greatest mortality among Goodhue County post offices. It closed on October 31, its mail sent to Cannon Falls. Later a Zumbrota rural route took care of the Hader patrons. Hader did not die at once. Although the blacksmith shops and similar trades went one by one out of business, the Haller store continued, and Joseph R. Tiller purchased it in 1920. After Erstad, Haugen & Company went out of business, Ohnstad and Larson bought the store, moved it across the road, and added it to their own building. On February 18, 1932, the two-story frame store burned, at a loss of $7,500 or more. Tiller promptly replaced it with a new two-story brick structure, 24 x 36 feet in floor area, which opened for business in June. This building fell to an explosion on August 18, 1945, that killed Edward Holt and his daughter Helen. The Holts were running the store for Tiller at the time. Rebuilt in 1946, the Hader store continued under Conrad Tiller and Ray Frederickson until 1960, when Duane Scharpen bought it. He and his wife, Mary, tended it until November 30, 1972.

For a time Hader had two stores. Walt Norby operated a gasoline filling station in the 1920s. Clifford Fox and I. O. Lund later took it over. They built an addition in 1940, and after the destruction of the Tiller store five years later, expanded it to a full-sized general store. A feed mill operated at least intermittently for many years. Chris Nygaard reportedly bought it from Bennie Moe and Andrew Hanson early in 1915. Whether this represented a lineal descendant of the feed mill reported in 1884 is unknown. Neither do we know how long it served the area after 1915.

For nearly 45 years the Hader community enjoyed the services of a local dairy plant. In 1919 a group of local farmers organized the Hader Cooperative Cheese Association and built a cheese factory. For many years the factory prospered. During the tenure of Kenneth Zeller (formerly of Fair Point) as cheesemaker, it won several awards for its excellent product. On December 1, 1956, Joe Hoidahl, who had managed the Nansen factory until its closing that year, replaced James Paulson as manager. At that time the co-op had 38 patrons. One of the last such plants to survive in rural Goodhue County, the Hader co-op long served as an example of how a small factory could meet the challenge of larger

Hader store, 1940. *RWM*

competition. Finally, it faltered too. After ceasing the manufacture of cheese early in 1963, it served for about a year as a collection and processing point for milk sold by members of the association. Then, at the beginning of 1964, the

The Hader cheese factory, 1954. *RWM*

association merged with the Goodhue Cooperative Creamery. About four years later Mohr & Sons of Cannon Falls, a dealer in motorcycle and lawn-mower sales and service purchased the building. This business did not last long, however, and Darryl Logan of Forest Mills acquired, then greatly altered and expanded, the building for a repair shop. A rural school, started at Hader in pioneer days, continued until the 1950s. Then, with consolidation bringing an end to the rural school districts, the last Hader school building, erected in 1904, was moved to Wanamingo,

The Hader of today bears little resemblance to that of the late 19th century. Still on a major route of travel, the hamlet has changed profoundly in appearance due to the highway now running through it. When U.S. 52 became a four-lane highway in the early 1960s, a house on the site of the old hotel (torn down in 1950) was razed, together with the trees and outbuildings surrounding it. The route of Goodhue County Highway 8 between the cheese factory and the stores also changed, making direct access between these two parts of Hader no longer possible. Its original streets ignored from the start, Hader has watched more recent construction pay little attention to the roads actually used. Far from a contender for the county seat, Hader is not even the "wide place in the road" noted by one citizen on a radio broadcast in 1954.

Hay Creek

Like Hader, Hay Creek has seen better days. Unlike the former, it was never platted with notions of metropolitan grandeur. It just grew up around a mill located near a major route of travel. Instead of 15 postmasters, it had one throughout its operation of nearly 28 years. Albert A. Burkard (Sr.) became postmaster on December 3, 1874, and held the position until August 30, 1902.

Although Hay Creek did not appear in the gazetteers until after its post office opened, a flour mill went up there in 1866. A settlement had grown up around it by 1870. The census for that year showed, in addition to the mill, the following tradesmen: cooper Michael Hartman, hotel keeper Joseph Schultz, tailor William Burgdorf, stonemason Henry Wolpers, and carpenter Caspar Friedemann. Besides several mill employees, the community also included the Rev. John Horst, a Lutheran clergyman. All these men were born in Germany.

The mill itself was comparatively small, using just two run of stone and a force of 30 horsepower. Its owners claimed an investment of $4,000, with $9,490 worth of wheat ground into flour the previous year. According to a Meyer family tradition (the Meyers started Meyer Machine, Inc., in Red Wing), John Hack built the mill and later went into partnership with George F. Meyer. Listed as Hack & Meyer in the 1870 census, the mill operated under George Meyer for many years. Plagued by washouts of the dam, the mill converted to steampower about 1880. The first engine proved too small; in 1883 a larger one

The Meyer mill at Hay Creek. *GCHS*

replaced it. Long after the mill proper was torn down (around the time of World War II), the smokestack, erected with the conversion to steam, remained.

Hay Creek (or "The Bend") grew rapidly during the 1870s. By 1878, when a gazetteer listed its population at 150, it contained the Meyer mill, a general store and hotel run by Albert A. Burkard (Sr.), three blacksmiths, three stone-masons, three carpenters, three shoemakers, a wagonmaker, a painter, a physician, and two churches—German Lutheran and German Methodist. All but one of the names are German; Hay Creek was—and is—a German community.

A saloonkeeper and a second physician appeared on the 1880 census. Soon after Albert A. Burkard (Sr.), an immigrant from Germany, moved from Red Wing in 1867, he started a hotel—"Goodhue County House"—not far from the Hack mill. He kept a small store there, too, and built an addition for a dance hall. About 1895 he built the brick store that still stands today. When the hotel closed its doors is unclear, but the building, long converted to a farmhouse, also remains.

Hay Creek continued for many years as a trading and manufacturing center. At one time it had a brewery (pictured in the 1874 Andreas atlas), and as late as 1894 it claimed the mill, the Burkard hotel and store, a butcher shop, three blacksmiths (one also a wagonmaker), three carpenters, two stonemasons, and a shoemaker, as well as the two churches and a district school built in 1889. By 1900, however, only Burkard, Meyer, and one blacksmith—Claus Muhlman— showed up in a business directory. In 1911 Joe Oelkers and Christ Tillman opened a second store. Apparently, it had a short life.

Hay Creek was a station on the old Duluth, Red Wing & Southern Railroad, later absorbed by the CGW. But for a time the main Red Wing-Zumbrota high-

Burkard's County Hotel at Hay Creek. *GCHS*

Burkard's Store at Hay Creek, 1953. *RWM*

Hay Creek depot. *GCHS*

way followed a different route, bypassing Hay Creek. The construction of T.H. 58 in 1932 brought the traffic back to the Hay Creek store too late to save the town. By then only the store, the Lutheran church, the district school, a small depot, and a dozen or so houses remained. Since then the depot has gone (the railroad itself abandoned in 1965), and the school (closed in 1955) has become a community hall. The church is still active, and several new houses have gone up in recent decades. The store,operated by the Burkard family for 72 years, was sold to James and De Wayne Dressen in 1967. With the aid of their brother, Leo Jr., and other members of the family, they transformed it to "Dressen's Saloon & General Mercantile," a replica of an Old West saloon. The Dressens also operate a campground across the road from the store. For many years one could see, at the end of a grass-grown lane west of the former site of the depot, the ruins of the old mill, its tall chimney largely intact. That too now is gone.

Holden
Not long after the Norwegians changed the name of the old election precinct of Dunkirk to Holden, a post office began operating in the northwestern part of the township. Its first career was brief. Established March 6, 1860, it closed the following June 18. Charles H. Nichols was the first postmaster. George M. Nichols followed on May 11. Not until June 4, 1867, did the Holden post office reopen, with Thomas E. Thompson postmaster. From then it continued until the advent of RFD. The shift from postmasters of American stock to those of

foreign birth occurred early at Holden. At least one of the Nicholses—George—was born in Maine. But Thompson, age 27 in 1870, was an immigrant from Norway who had opened a store late in the previous decade.

The original Holden post office probably operated in the northeast quarter of section 7, where George Nichols made a claim in November 1858. Upon the appointment of postmaster Thomas E. Lajord on May 9, 1871, the revived post office operated in his store, in the southwestern corner of section 4. Since Thomas E. Thompson and Thomas E. Lajord probably were one and the same, the office may have been there before 1870. A Lutheran church, predecessor of the present Vang church a mile north, served in the extreme southwest corner of the section. Lajord's store was just east of it. In 1872 there was also a blacksmith shop run by J. O. Berget. An 1877 map shows a wagon shop and a shoe shop at this crossroads. An 1878 gazetteer lists a store (Lajord's), a hotel, a blacksmith, a wagonmaker, a boot- and shoemaker, a painter, a tailor, and a physician within the service area of the Holden post office. Probably not all of them lived in the village proper, population 50.

On March 6, 1879, the post office passed to Knute T. Rogne, who held it little more than a year until John J. Stene of Stene & Glemme, general store proprietors, took over on June 21, 1880. A gazetteer published that year also lists John E. Widmey, the tailor two years earlier, as running a general store. Rogne showed up as a shoemaker (as earlier) and H. O. Hamand as blacksmith and wagonmaker. Holden by this time had 35 residents.

The postmaster with the longest record of service at Holden was Augun H. Brokke, appointed on January 23, 1882. He held the office until April 23, 1901, followed by John E. Widmey. During those two decades, the hamlet appears to have declined gradually, as the township lost population and the need for a rural trading center diminished. By 1884 the gazetteer listed only Brokke and Hamand in the gazetteer, though Widmey probably remained at the hamlet too. By 1886 J. Kolstad appeared as storekeeper. The post office may have moved from place to place as it changed hands, but an 1894 county atlas and an 1898 Site Location Survey report show it as in 1877—in section 4, east of the present cemetery. By 1894, however, the store operated on the northeast corner of section 8, where the Widmey family ran it later.

The Holden post office gave way to RFD on October 31, 1903, after which the hamlet gradually lost its identity. Because of a shift northward in the center of the Norwegian population, the Vang church was rebuilt in 1896 on the north line of the township. Only the cemetery marks the old site. In 1904 John Widmey sold out the stock in his store and settled down to farming. Less than two years later he reportedly intended to return to his old stand and "continue his business as formerly." There is no record of such a return, however, and Widmey's granddaughter, born in 1904, had no recollection of a store in the building, where she resided in 1964. Now that building is gone. The name of the community survives on a decorative sign at a large house across the road, in the southeast corner of section 5. It says "The Holden House 1884." That, a new house, and the cemetery are all that remain of Holden.

Lena

When the Rochester & Northern Minnesota railway built its line from Rochester to Zumbrota in 1878, it also established a station called New Jerusalem in the northern part of Pine Island township. The name apparently was changed almost at once to Lena, for reasons unknown. A rural schoolhouse already stood in the southwest corner of section 3, and soon the Van Dusen Elevator Company erected a grain warehouse. On January 6, 1879, a post office opened at Lena, with Myron F. Coleman postmaster. Like Aurland and Finney, the Lena post office came and went in a matter of months. It closed on August 4 of the same year. Since none of the nearby towns had newspapers of which copies exist today, the brief career of the Lena post office has dropped into an oblivion more complete than that of almost any other office in the county.

Lena lasted longer than its post office. Commonly referred to as Lena Station, it was a trading point rather than a community. Even as a railroad station it received only minimal attention in its early years. As late as 1892 there was no depot at Lena. Passengers boarding the train there had to wait in a "small house" owned by the Van Dusen elevator. Someone persuaded the company to keep a fire in the building in February of that year. About that time Thomas

Lena cheese factory, 1940. *RWM*

Morgan started a stage line between Lena and Mazeppa. By this means the people of Mazeppa could make rail connections to Rochester without having to go to Zumbrota on the narrow-gauge line. (The *Pine Island Journal* had suggested such a service in 1890.) In 1900 there was talk of putting up a depot at Lena. The Chicago & North Western Railway, which took over the Rochester & Northern Minnesota almost immediately after construction of its line, apparently did so.

In 1901 the Duluth, Red Wing & Southern became part of the CGW system, which the next year built an extension from Zumbrota to Rochester, parallel to the earlier line. The extension began service in January 1903, making a stop at the neat new little depot at Lena. Described by the *Mazeppa Tribune*, "as nobby a little building as can be found anywhere," it contained an operating room, a waiting room, and a small storage room. Lena remained an agency station until early in 1918, when the CGW railroad dispensed with its agent. There was such an outcry that the company reportedly considered reopening it, but it never did so.

About the time the CGW depot appeared, Lena enjoyed the services of two grain warehouses. Before many years it would acquire a cheese factory. During the second decade of the 20th century, cheese factories sprouted up across the southeastern part of the county.[6] In March of 1917 a group of farmers organized the Lena Dairy Association and erected a frame building (later stuccoed), 22 by 32 feet, just west of the railroad track in the northeast corner of

Not much more than a sign, Lena in 1941. *RWM*

section 9. The original proprietors were Martin M. Anderson, Ole T. Gullickson, William Manthei, and Ole H. Haugen.

The cheese factory outlived Lena's other business places as well as the depot (or depots). In 1926 it had 12 patrons and made 300 pounds of cheese daily, sold through the Wisconsin Cheese Producers Federation. Operated in its later years by Edgar A. and Arthur W. Parkin of Pine Island, the Lena factory closed its doors on March 9, 1941. When the highway (T.H. 60) was widened in 1946, the building was torn down. The depot, removed about 1938, gave way to a sign along the track, itself abandoned in 1965. A schoolhouse built in 1941 served for only a decade. Converted to a dwelling, it alone remains at the former site of Lena.

Miami

Among the more obscure early post offices is Miami, established March 12, 1858, with Elam Pease postmaster. On November 22 of that year Samuel Carpenter succeeded Pease and retained the office until it closed October 16, 1860. The location, at least during Carpenter's term, was in the northeast quarter of section 28, Warsaw township, where he had made a claim in August 1856. This is about a half-mile south of the later hamlet of Wangs. The Sewall map of 1857 places Miami approximately at this location.

Both Pease and Carpenter appear in Warsaw township records as local officials about 1860. A well-driller by occupation but also a prosperous farmer, Pease was elected supervisor and justice of the peace in 1858. Carpenter was elected supervisor in 1859, served for several years, and was chosen overseer of the poor in 1865. Pease evidently did not remain long in Warsaw township, for in October 1860 he made a claim in section 2 of Holden. Listed in the 1860 census as age 42, he was originally from Ohio (which has a Miami River), had lived in Wisconsin before moving to Minnesota, and currently owned $800 worth of real estate. During the Civil War he moved away. Carpenter, a native of New York, was then 58 and apparently had real estate valued at $6,000.

Minneola

Some time after the western half of Zumbrota township split off to form a separate political unit, a post office bearing the name of the new township opened. The first postmaster, appointed May 11, 1863, appears in the postal records as Albra Troombly. Elsewhere the name is *Twombly* or *Twombley*. About age 39 at the time, he was a native of Maine who had come to Minnesota by way of New York State, where three of his eight children were born, and New Hampshire, where another was born. In October 1860 he took a claim in the northeast quarter of section 22. This places the original site of the post office near where the Minneola township hall (a former church building) now stands.

On September 12, 1864, Jabez Bradley Locke became postmaster and presumably moved the office to his home on the hill, half a mile or so northwest of the former site. Locke, who also served in the state legislature, lived along the St. Paul-Dubuque road and kept a diary. There he recorded incidents occurring along that avenue of travel. At least one history credits him with establishing the post office in the first place. Arthur Tappen replaced him as postmaster on April 12, 1871. On the following August 8 the office closed. Tappen, then 22, appeared in the 1870 census as a member of the Twombly household, apparently a relative of Mrs. Louisa Twombly. The Minneola post office served a wide area, so its early close is puzzling. No town or village ever developed around it.

Although Minneola was the only post office in the township of that name, a hamlet called Barr grew up around a clay plant started by Ed Barr of Austin in section 21, near the center of the township. As noted earlier, commercially exploitable deposits of clay underlie much of Goodhue County. As early as 1906 a clay plant operated on section 22, about a mile and a half east of where the Barr plant went up in 1910–11. Originally known as the Zumbrota Clay Manufacturing Company, this firm had, like the Barr enterprise, a checkered career. Reorganized on March 13, 1913, as the Zumbrota Brick and Tile Company, it later operated with the Barr plant, closing with it in 1932.

According to the Minneola township history in *Zumbrota: The First 100 Years,* Ed Barr began prospecting for clay in the spring of 1910. Finding a suitable deposit on the Andrew Olson farm, he bought the land and began erecting a T-shaped building 350 by 50 by 60 feet that year. He planned for 20 kilns but built only 12. As many as 300 men and 50 teams, mostly mules, worked on the construction. Most of the laborers were Mexicans who lived in tents along the Zumbro River. The Milwaukee railroad ran a spur from its track on the south side of the river, first to bring construction materials to the site and later to carry away the products of the plant. One could still see remnants of the bridge in 1981, two years after the closing of the line. For many years a small depot stood beside the tracks, across the river from the plant.

Besides the clay plant, the company erected a boardinghouse to accommodate 40 men, as well as a small general store and nine two-room cottages—all during the first year of plant operation. The boardinghouse contained such amenities as a pool table and a dance floor. By the time the plant was in full swing in the fall of 1911, a village (more accurately a company town) had sprung up on the north side of the Zumbro.

The Barr clay plant did not succeed. Ed Barr apparently left it early in its career, after which the company underwent a bewildering succession of reorganizations and changes of ownership. Still named the Barr Brick & Tile Company when articles of incorporation were filed with the state auditor on July 22, 1913, it later emerged as the Colburn Brick & Tile Company. The Great Depression brought final failure to the enterprise in 1932. Some people who continued to live in the company houses found employment on Works Progress Administration (WPA) projects and the like. Olaf J. Peterson bought the property in 1937, and from 1950 to 1955 he processed clay for sale to the Red Wing Pottery for red flower pots. He gradually dismantled the main building and sold the salvageable brick and tile.

When the author first visited Barr in May 1938, much of the plant was intact. Two years later, when he photographed the place, there was still a great deal to see. As the years passed, however, the building, kilns, and smokestacks vanished bit by bit. Pictures taken in the early 1950s show some of the houses still occupied, as well as remnants of the plant. Less has been visible each year since then, less to suggest the ambitious endeavors of Ed Barr and his successors in the early 20th century. Four of the houses are still occupied, but in summer nothing of the plant is visible from the road.

In the mid-1960s Peterson began development of what became the Shades of Sherwood campground, in the vicinity of the old clay plant. In 1966 a Minneapolis firm reportedly considered building a cement-mix factory on the site. Nothing came of this idea, though the county planning commission took it seriously enough to investigate the proposed operation as a possible source of pollution in the Zumbro River, five miles above Zumbrota. In 1976 the *Zumbrota News* published a postcard picture of the clay plant as it appeared in its heyday. Regard this as its valedictory.

Nansen

Like Aurland, the Nansen post office arrived when the show was almost over. Opened just a few years before the start of RFD, it had a short career. One postmaster—Ole H. Pynten—served at Nansen, in Holden township, starting May 7, 1898. The office, probably named for Arctic explorer Fridtjof Nansen, was in Pynten's general store, in the southwest quarter of the northeast quarter of section 12. Pynten, referred to as the "Cannon Valley merchant," opened his store as early as 1892. According to his report to the Post Office Department before establishment of the office, it would serve about 90 people. The office closed January 14, 1905, one of the last in the county replaced by RFD then.

Nansen was never a village of much consequence, but it boasted two business places for many years. Pynten died in 1906; John Ohnstad of Cannon Falls then rented the store. Ohnstad did not remain long. By the end of the year L. H. Pynten, brother of the deceased storekeeper, reportedly sold the store, and the 80-acre farm on which it stood, to Thomas B. Thompson, who opened it for business in February 1907. Six years later he was still operating it, but by 1926 Hans Underdahl ran the store. It burned down during a heat wave in July 1936.

Nansen's second business was a cheese factory, started in the spring of 1904 by John Klossner, formerly cheesemaker at Sogn. Privately operated

Nansen cheese factory, 1953. *RWM*

for several years, the factory became the object of an attempt by local farmers who wished to form a cooperative in 1913. Storekeeper T. B. Thompson, bought it, however. Not until 1921 did a farmers' group gain possession. The Nansen Cooperative Dairy Association opened for business March 10, 1921, and ran with success for some years. In 1926 it had 22 patrons, and by 1938 the membership had increased to more than 50. Eventually it lost out to competition from larger concerns. It closed in 1956, and its electric service ceased on December 4 of that year. The building is now a private residence.

Norway

As mentioned in connection with the Eidsvold post office, the center of Norwegian settlement in Goodhue County was in western Wanamingo and eastern Holden townships. There on June 1, 1857, the Norway post office opened with Ole Olson postmaster. The original location was in section 24 of Holden, along a state road laid out in 1856. It soon moved across the line into section 19 of Wanamingo. Never platted as a town, Norway remained throughout its history a rural post office and small trading center. Its second postmaster was Ole D. Huset, appointed on February 8, 1865. Butler Johnson, listed as proprietor of a store at Norway in an 1872 gazetteer, followed on April 15, 1867. Johnson appeared as a grocer, age 26, in the 1870 census.

The postmaster who served longest was Botolf J. Borlaug, appointed on May 14, 1873. Pictured in an 1874 atlas, the store housing the post office long

A family farmhouse at Norway. *GCHS*

served as an emporium for farmers' trade over a wide area. It was known as the Borlaug store long after the postmaster of that name left in 1891 to become a banker in Kenyon. In the early years of Borlaug's term, Norway was the address of a blacksmith, a shoemaker, and a physician—Christian Gronvold. An 1877 map shows Borlaug's store just north of the road (now Goodhue County Highway 8), on the west line of Wanamingo township. On the south side of the road, a little to the east, was the shoe shop, and across the town line, also south of the road, was the blacksmith shop.

The original Norway store, built about 1870, burned on July 16, 1886. The owner promptly rebuilt, and the new store opened for business that fall. Upon Borlaug's departure in 1891, Peter O. Floan took charge, becoming postmaster on May 9. About this time the Crescent Creamery opened a milk separator there. Dr. Gronvold and a blacksmith were still in business at that time. The post office passed into the hands of Knut S. Groven on May 15, 1896, but O. S. Holmquist apparently ran the store. In the fall of 1896 he sold his stock to Ole H. Huset, who became postmaster on November 22.

Norway was nearly finished by then. A new postmaster, Nicolai O. Huset, appointed August 29, 1901, served only until the post office closed on March 15, 1902. The store did not long survive it. In May 1905 the *Red Wing Republican* reported that W. W. Ronningen had bought the four-acre lot containing the store from Borlaug, who was going to remove the building. Although this news item remarked on how desolate the site would look "after the old land mark that has been there for the last 35 years, shall have disappeared," the building had stood there fewer than 20 years.

Today there is nothing at the site of Norway to suggest the hamlet there earlier. Open fields occupy the store corner, and no trace of other business places remains.

Poplar Grove

One of the early inland post offices, its brief history obscured by the passage of time, was Poplar Grove, established October 16, 1855, in the northern part of Pine Island township. Its first postmaster, John Lee, ran a hotel on the route of the St. Paul and Dubuque stage line. The exact location is unclear, as modern roads do not follow that trail. Lee made a claim in the southeast quarter of section 9 in July 1857, however, and he may have occupied the land before recording the claim. This would place the site south and a little west of the later post office of Lena. Poplar Grove appears on the Sewall and on the slightly later Morris and Von Minden maps.

Joseph N. Dodson, who lived in the eastern part of section 15, followed Lee as postmaster on May 24, 1858. Truman Parker, who earlier had been postmaster at Sunapee, succeeded Dodson on May 5, 1860. Parker, a native of New York, had settled in Roscoe township in the late 1850s and then moved, early in 1860, to Pine Island, where he went into the hotel business. The next postmaster was James Pratt, appointed December 31, 1861. He served until the office closed the following April 6. The Poplar Grove post office probably changed location during its six-and-a-half years, but at least the first two postmasters lived along the route of the stage line, an important road throughout this period. An 1877 map shows a diagonal road, now vanished, extending from section 6 about to the center of the township. A farm lane in section 9 still follows a small portion of this road, and in the extreme southeast corner of the township a local road follows a longer stretch of the old trail.

Poplar Grove Lutheran Church, 1953. *RWM*

Although the post office of Poplar Grove has been gone more than 140 years, the name persists. On February 14, 1911, a group of local farmers organized the "Poplar Grove Dairy Association" and soon thereafter erected a cheese factory on the south line of section 8. All trace of this factory has long since vanished, but a German Lutheran church known locally as Poplar Grove Church long stood in section 14. Built in 1877, the first St. Peter's Church was replaced in 1920. The congregation dissolved in 1986, and the building was torn down in 1989.

Rest Island

In the early 1890s a resident of Central Point township worked to establish a colony for inebriates along Lake Pepin. John G. Woolley, a one-time alcoholic and later candidate for president on the Prohibitionist ticket, in 1891 acquired land on the lakeshore. He managed to interest some Minneapolis temperance people to the extent that they offered considerable financial support. His chief backers were Mrs. E. A. Russell, operator of a temperance restaurant in Minneapolis, and Etta Thompson, a young woman of means, prominent in the Methodist church. With their assistance, Woolley had several cottages built at Rest Island and started a farm through which he hoped the colony would become at least partly self-supporting.

The big years for Rest Island were 1892 and 1893. In the former year a large hotel, variously called the Hotel Russell, Russell Inn, and Russell Pavilion, went up. Construction on Willard Cottage, named for suffragette and temperance leader Frances E. Willard, also began. Rest Island issued its own souvenir, complete with pictures of Lake City and the facility as it then existed. Although Miss Willard did not appear as planned for the dedication of the cottage named for her, a bevy of prominent temperance people, including many clergymen, predominantly Methodist, attended a convention there that summer, formally launching the project. In Washington the previous April, Woolley had campaigned for the establishment of a post office at Rest Island. The next month, on May 26, 1892, Harry N. Timolat, superintendent of the Rest Island enterprise, became postmaster. He retained the position until August 24, 1893, when Woolley succeeded him.

For a time Woolley's experiment seemed to be meeting with success. Despite high water in Lake Pepin, which flooded much of the island, and the failure of contributions to meet expectations, the undertaking continued through the remainder of 1892 and well into 1893. Woolley was absent for much of this time while on a lecture tour in England. The *Lake City Graphic-Sentinel*, whose editor was sympathetic, chronicled Woolley's travels as well as the events at Rest Island. In May 1893 the first issue of a periodical called *The Rest Islander* appeared. It consisted of 12 pages of four columns each, three pages filled with advertisements of Minneapolis and Lake City business firms. It was to appear monthly at a subscription rate of one dollar per year. It survived through only seven issues, for by November the whole Rest Island project had collapsed.

The causes for the failure of Woolley's colony were primarily economic. Contributions began to fall off as the Panic of 1893 spread and money became scarce. Although the colony had pledges of $2,000 to complete Willard Cottage, it received only $1,269 in cash. The 1893 summer convention was not so well attended as in previous years, and contributions no doubt were fewer than before. Then Woolley came under attack for alleged misappropriation of funds. Early in October he defended himself at meetings in Lake City and Minneapolis. A committee appointed to investigate the financial affairs of Rest Island found disbursements of $23,297.79 and receipts of $19,636.73. Woolley had made up the deficiency of $3,661.06 from personal earnings from his lecture tours in the United States and abroad. He had nothing to do with the $1,201.23 contributed by Minneapolis women for Willard Cottage or with the $827 contributed by Lake City people for grading ground and roads at the colony.

But Woolley and his enterprise were deeply in debt and hard pressed by creditors. In November he turned over his property at Rest Island to Etta Thompson. Two tracts not included in this transfer were to be sold, with proceeds devoted to the liquidation of Woolley's personal debts. Apparently the colony vacated the premises soon afterward, for on December 30, 1893, the Rest Island post office closed. Thus ended one of Goodhue County's most interesting experiments.

The Rest Island site later hosted a summer resort. It continued as a site for annual interdenominational religious conventions for several years. Work on Willard Cottage resumed in the spring of 1894. In June a reception for Miss Thompson entertained 175 people. A newspaper reported that she and Mrs. Russell were "making the Island one of the most delightful spots on earth for those desiring rest and comfort during the hot season." Miss Thompson reportedly spent $30,000 or more on improvements at Rest Island— erecting cottages and laying out parks, lawns, drives, and boulevards. She reluctantly substituted a ten-cent admission fee for the free-will offerings customarily taken at various meetings, so as to sustain, at least in part, the convention that summer. With excursion steamer *Ethel Howard* making daily trips on the lake, the concern allowed camping privileges all summer. In general, Rest Island promoted itself as a commercial resort with strong religious overtones. In the spring of 1896 it was surveyed and platted, with the intention of selling lots on which summer residents might build cottages. Whatever success this venture may have met with, the project petered out, the plat was vacated in 1911, and most of Rest Island thereafter reverted to brush and woodland.

Roscoe

Three Goodhue County hamlets have somewhat parallel histories. Hader, Roscoe, and Wastedo all were platted in the summer of 1857. All acquired post offices the same year, and none achieved the proportions expected by their founders. Still, all of them developed into rural trading centers. None ever received a railroad, but all survived as crossroads hamlets, with at least one active business place as late as 1964. Of the three, Roscoe was the least ambitiously projected, but it remains the only one with no part of the original plat vacated.

The founders of Roscoe were Fletcher Hagler and Jacob R. Good, who came to the county in 1856 (one source says 1855) to make claims in Roscoe township. Hagler's was the northwest quarter of section 29. Good's was an adjoining tract in section 30. Both filed claims on June 20, 1857, but probably they had occupied the land long before that. According to the earliest county history, the two men promptly built and stocked a general store, probably on Hagler's claim. Then or in the following year they opened a hotel, possibly in the same building. In the spring of 1857 John G. Hepner started a blacksmith shop, apparently on Good's claim west of the later site of the Roscoe school.

The next step in promotion of the village was a survey of streets and blocks. This accomplished, the plat was recorded July 9, 1857. This village plat, of which Hagler and Good were proprietors, was much less extensive than those of Hader and Wastedo. Occupying a few acres in the northwest corner of section 29 and the northeast corner of section 30, it contained only 11 numbered blocks and a public square. Besides the road (now Goodhue County Highway 11) that formed its northern boundary, it had a principal street named Broadway (now Goodhue County Highway 27) and six other streets. Probably none of these secondary streets was ever graded for use.

Having platted the town, Hagler next set about getting a post office. On October 14, 1857, Roscoe post office started with Fletcher Hagler postmaster. He held the job less than three months. Oliver Webb replaced him on January 6, 1858, and remained postmaster nearly ten years.

Though treated by later county historians as a casualty of the Panic of 1857, Roscoe seems to have been thriving in June 1858, when the editor of the *Red Wing Republican* visited it on a tour of the county. After describing a stop in Zumbrota, he wrote:

> The end of another day's journey found us partaking of the hospitalities of mine hosts of the Roscoe Hotel, Messrs. Hagler and Good. These gentlemen are the original proprietors of the town site of Roscoe, to whose enterprise our county is indebted for one of the many flourishing communities in her possession. This village, though young and of very modest pretentions [*sic*], is possessor of all the elements of a substantial prosperity

and future growth. In the hands of its present inhabitants it is destined to become a point of no mean importance. Surrounded by an extensive agricultural region already under improvement, Roscoe is made the center of a considerable trade. It is at the junction of several important State roads and mail routes, on which there is a constant stream of travel. Stores, hotels, schools, & c., are among the "institutions" of the place.

If the Mitchell history can be trusted, Hagler and Good closed their store shortly after this editorial visit, for they are said to have run it about two years. Except for its location on a main road—and even that was not so much an advantage as the *Republican* article pretended—Roscoe had no special features to ensure its prosperity. On the open prairie, it had no waterpower in a period when mill sites were an important consideration in locating towns. Every major Goodhue County town surviving from the time before railroads is located on a stream capable of turning mill wheels. Hence Mitchell said of Roscoe: "Though a village in embryo and a city in prospect, it never assumed more gigantic proportions than a small hamlet of a dozen houses."

He made the comment in 1869, when Hepner's blacksmith shop apparently was Roscoe's only business. George Hoagland had taken over its post office on October 5, 1867. The office closed November 30, 1868, and reopened 16 days later, with Fletcher Hagler once again postmaster. Hagler, born in Illinois in 1824, served several terms as justice of the peace in Roscoe township, captained a home-guard organization called the Roscoe Mounted Militia during the Dakota Conflict (Sioux Uprising) of 1862, and served again as an officer in the First Minnesota Artillery late in the Civil War. In 1869 he moved to Cherry Grove and in 1875 to Pine Island, where he later became postmaster. He died in 1898. Upon his departure from Roscoe, the post office passed to Hepner on December 23, 1869. He continued for about five years until on December 8, 1874, August Buchholz succeeded him.

During all of this time Roscoe village appears to have been in the doldrums. Prospects improved in 1877, however, when Martin L. Webb opened a store on the northwest corner of section 29. He became postmaster on May 10 of that year. Besides Hepner's blacksmith shop, there was by this time another such business run by Joseph Elliott in the southwest corner of section 20, about where the Roscoe store later stood. An 1878 gazetteer lists the district school, a Methodist church, and carpenter Casper Schneebeli. By 1880 John Miller and Alfred Rogers had replaced Schneebeli and Elliott. Rogers also served as wagonmaker. In 1882 Webb seems to have sold out to Harvey Catlin, formerly at Ayr, three miles west. Catlin (a.k.a. J. Harvey Catlin and Joseph H. Catlin) became postmaster on February 8. Rogers had left by this time, and Hepner conducted the only blacksmithing business.

During the nine years the Ayr post office was out of operation, the gazetteers listed at least some of the tradesmen who had received mail there under the Roscoe post office. Thus in 1884 the Roscoe list includes blacksmith J. N. Nessen—presumably the Jacob N. Nesson who had served as postmaster at Ayr. By 1888 he was the only blacksmith on the list; Hepner apparently had died or retired by then. Whether Hepner, 66 at the time of the 1880 census, continued his business much after that date is unknown. Although gazetteers for 1884–85 and 1886–87 list his name, the Roscoe correspondent of the *Pine Island Journal* as early as 1883 issued a plea for "a good, reliable blacksmith at Roscoe, the late blacksmith Mr. P. B. Townsend having removed to Pine Island." Catlin that spring was brightening the inside of his store. Roscoe nearly always had a blacksmith during the period, though the gazetteers did not invariably list one.

In the later 1880s a literary or debating society relieved the monotony of winter at Roscoe. The society met in the schoolhouse to discuss such topics as "Resolved, that Dakota should be admitted into the Union as two states" or "Resolved, that the railroads and telegraphs should be owned by the United States government" or "Resolved, that women should have the right of suffrage." On the whole, the topics debated at Roscoe seem to have been more contemporary and political than those discussed at Hader about the same time. At Hader the debates ran more to "Resolved, that novels are more injurious than beneficial" and "Resolved, that wealth does not tend to elevate the human character." A committee of three judges decided the winning side.

In 1890 a group of local farmers organized a stock company and erected a cream separator at a cost of $500. Although the farmers owned the building, the machinery was the property of the Crescent Creamery Company. By the end of May it was handling 850 gallons a day. A fire in February 1892 destroyed the building, but the company promptly rebuilt it. A feed mill in operation by this time was by 1896 in the hands of E. C. Anderson. Catlin sold his store to the firm of Carlson and Hibbard in 1892, and John W. Carlson became postmaster on May 13 of that year. He was removed late the next year, following a complaint by a former patron. Charged with detaining a letter, he was found innocent, and the *Pine Island Record* denounced his accuser as a "deadbeat" who had left for parts unknown. Nevertheless, Carlson's partner, George F. Hibbard took over the post office on December 6, 1893. Hibbard continued to run store and post office after the partnership dissolved in 1896.

Roscoe had a succession of blacksmiths. C. B. Gibson, who served briefly in that capacity, moved away late in 1893. Edward Hegness of Moland started a blacksmith shop in the spring of 1896, but upon the outbreak of the Spanish-American War he left to join Company C at Zumbrota. He returned, however, and other blacksmiths followed; as long as horses were widely used, there was a blacksmithy at Roscoe. The old building, on the west side of the road south of the school, did not come down until the 1940s. In the middle 1890s Jacob Andrist, according to gazetteers as late as 1900, operated a hotel there as well.

Despite general satisfaction with Hibbard as postmaster, an 1897 report suggested that because he was a Democrat he would lose the job upon McKinley's election. In December came announcement of Tollef O. Sundry's appointment to the position. Though the rumor was essentially correct, Sundry was not appointed until February 3, 1898. Meanwhile, farmers of the area apparently had become dissatisfied with the service afforded by the Crescent Creamery. Early in 1898 they held a meeting to organize a cooperative and elect a board of managers. They did not find it necessary to enter active competition with the company, for late in March the creamery burned. The "Roscoe Butter & Cheese Factory" operated out of a reconstructed building there by early May.

The post office changed hands twice more before it closed. On August 8, 1900, Andrew Finstuen became postmaster. Nelson O. Romness, of the firm Romness Brothers then running the store, succeeded Finstuen the next February 2. By this time the store was located in the southwest corner of section 20, where it remained. The post office outlasted most of the rural offices off the railroads, but it finally closed on January 14, 1905.

Soon thereafter, Nels Romness went to Wanamingo to run a branch store, and his brother Halvor took sole charge of the store at Roscoe. In July 1907 the store and adjacent residence burned to the ground, with a loss of more than $5,000, only $800 covered by insurance. Despite first reports that Romness Brothers would not rebuild, the store was replaced, and it continued to serve the area until 1984. For many years Otto Peterson ran the store. He sold it in 1937

Roscoe store, 1977. *RWM*

to Knute Lien. Mr. and Mrs. Virgil Henschel operated it from 1946 until 1978, when they sold it to Bob and Judy (Purdy) Richardson of Pine Island. The store held a "grand opening" November 24, 25, and 26. Judy's parents, George and Dorothy Purdy, moved there from Indiana in 1979 and ran the store for the next few years. Closed in 1984, the building was torn down by May 17, 1997.

The Roscoe Dairy Association, successor to the earlier farmers' cooperative, organized in June 1918. The cheese factory on the hill east of the village stayed in business for many years but began to lose patronage in the 1930s. When Goodhue County Cooperative Electric extended its lines to Roscoe in 1938, the factory was temporarily out of operation. Later reopened, it suspended operations again in the winter of 1942–43, only to revive again the following summer. With business declining, it closed its doors for good in 1949. The district school continued until the early 1950s, when consolidated schools supplanted it. The building became a dwelling, later stood empty, and finally fell to the wrecking ball.

Today Roscoe has seven houses and the old cheese-factory building, used for a time as a repair shop. If the village has not realized the dreams of its original proprietors, neither has it vanished.

Roscoe Centre

Successor to the Sunapee post office, Roscoe Centre opened on August 12, 1863, with Silas W. Rice postmaster. Rice, age 29, had come west from New York State with his father, Constant Rice, who owned considerable real and personal property at the time of the 1860 census. Three years later, on July 26, 1866, William P. Smith succeeded Silas Rice and retained the office 16 years. Born in New York about 1815, Smith was a substantial farmer who also operated a general store and hotel in the southwest corner of the northwest quarter of section 10, Roscoe township, a few rods east of today's Stordahl Lutheran Church. In 1878, the year the church organized, John O. Hanson was running a blacksmith shop south of the road (now Goodhue County Highway 12). Hanson and an assistant, Nels Pearson, also appear in the 1880 census. This may have been all the business activity at Roscoe Centre at that time. By 1882 Smith no longer appeared in the *Minnesota State Gazetteer*. On December 18 of that year the post office closed.

Although the annals of Roscoe Center (current spelling) are simple, they are not so short as the early loss of the post office might suggest. The Stordahl congregation survived and flourishes today. After the old church fell to a windstorm, the present brick structure went up in 1915. Business activity returned to Roscoe Center early in the 20th century with the organization in October 1912 of the Roscoe Center Butter & Cheese Association. It served the area for more than half a century. Surviving several crises, it was the last rural cheese factory in the county to go out of business. With only 17 patrons in 1949, it

The factory of the Roscoe Center Butter & Cheese Association, 1952. *RWM*

closed down for more than a year, then pulled out of the slump and by 1962 increased its patronage to 50. Severely damaged by fire in 1959, the factory on the site of the old blacksmith shop was partially rebuilt and greatly altered in appearance. In the end, however, it went the way of the other cheese factories, ceasing operation in the summer of 1966. The next April the cement block building, 30 x 48 feet, and an adjacent three-bedroom house went up for sale.

Never platted as a town, never more than a crossroads hamlet, Roscoe Center nevertheless contributed to the history of Goodhue County and, through its active church, continues to do so.

Ryan

The entry for the Black Oak post office (see page 25) mentions the appearance in an 1882 gazetteer of boot-and-shoe merchant Philip Ryan. On July 12 of that year the Ryan post office opened with Philip Ryan postmaster. Ryan's store, which carried general merchandise as well as boots and shoes, was in section 14 of Belle Creek township, just north of St. Columbkill's Catholic Church. Although Ryan and Black Oak were less than three miles apart, both post offices operated until 1885, when the latter closed.

Philip Ryan was a member of one of the largest families in the Irish colony that started with the arrival of the Doyles in the early days of settlement. St. Columbkill's parish organized there and built a church in 1865. The church, the store, and a knot of half-a-dozen houses made up a hamlet that made no effort to become a town. In 1892 a new church went up, and the old building became

Elizabeth and Phil Ryan with children Sarah, Jim, and Catherine at the Ryan post office, Belle Creek township. The village disappeared from the map in 1939. *GCHS*

a meeting hall. Declared unsafe in 1907, it was torn down and replaced by a new one fitted with the latest conveniences, including gasoline lighting. It served the community until the 1930s.

Ryan remained in charge of the post office that bore his name for more than 20 years. Then, on September 4, 1902, Reuben J. Steffa, who had bought the store from him earlier that year, became postmaster. Steffa served less than six months before the office closed, February 28, 1903. The store apparently went out of business about the same time. Local newspapers did not mention it after that date. In 1910 a fire destroyed some sheds, a barn full of hay, the church stables, and "Phil Ryan's old house"—presumably the store building. Ryan today consists of the church, the adjacent cemetery, and a single farmhouse. The name is rarely used (the U.S. Geological Survey places it in the northeast quarter of section 15), its post office and trading center mostly forgotten.

Skyberg
Although it later developed into a village of local importance, Skyberg began with only a post office. About 1877 Simon O. Skyberg, an immigrant from Norway, and Dr. Ole Abelson opened a general store in the northwest corner of section 36, Kenyon township. At first they received mail from Fair Point, the nearest post office. In 1878 a citizens' petition to the Post Office Department requested a post office to serve residents of the area around the new store. On February 17, 1879, Abelson became postmaster at the new office of Skyberg.

At this stage, Skyberg could scarcely be called a village; neither did it become one until the arrival of the railroad in 1885. A blacksmith, a carpenter, and a dressmaker listed their addresses as Skyberg in 1880, however. Soon thereafter Edwin H. Ells opened a second store there. He became postmaster on November 18, 1881. Ells's store seems to have been several rods east of the first one but still some distance west of the later railway village. Ells was among the earliest settlers in the vicinity and has more claim than even S. O. Skyberg to fatherhood of the village, for he platted it some years later. Both men retired from business but remained in the locality until about 1920. Both died in the early 1930s.

Skyberg did not suddenly become a town when the railroad arrived in 1885. A depot (apparently not much of a building) for "Skyburg" appeared, and a milk station was in business by 1888. But a gazetteer of that year listed only the two stores plus carpenter and dressmaker. Ells seems also to have run some sort of hotel and eating place—the Skyberg House—within a few years after the rail service arrived. By the early 1890s, things were looking up. In response to local demand, the railroad put in a new depot in 1891, and later that year a grain warehouse went up along a newly constructed sidetrack. Talk of a new store culminated late in 1892 or early the next year in newcomer Francis J. White's establishment, near the tracks. On November 15, 1893, White became postmaster, a position he held for nearly 30 years.

By 1895 Skyberg was riding the wave of its first boom. The *Kenyon Leader* remarked: "Many new buildings have been erected here this summer," without specificity. June of that year saw the survey for a town plat, unrecorded until January 13. 1897. Modest in comparison with the plats of 40 years earlier, it provided for only one street and two blocks, one divided into 12 lots extending from the unnamed street.

Skyberg had a blacksmith off and on during these years, and in 1897 Robert Stephenson and Alex McCadden set up a shop that remained in business for some time. The year 1897 also saw establishment of the Skyberg Cooperative Creamery Association, after several years of abortive proposals. The formal opening of the creamery, on July 31, was a gala event, with a picnic, a band concert, a baseball game, speakers, and even an attempt to immortalize the occasion in verse. The creamery, in operation about 50 years, was early on a successful enterprise, a principal source of Skyberg's economic importance.

Before the turn of the century, several other businesses enhanced the economic life of the community. In 1898 the Ayr merchants, Layng and Barsness, moved their store to Skyberg; later they started a lumberyard. A livery stable and a new grain elevator opened the next year, and both stores expanded. At some undetermined time, both of the earlier stores had gone out of business. Activity now concentrated at the village platted by Ells, who surveyed a large addition to the plat in 1899. The addition encompassed a new street, an alley, and 16 lots.

Soon after the turn of the century a hardware store opened, and in 1902 the businessmen erected a two-story building, its upper floor for use as a hall. Upon dedication of the building on August 20, the *Leader* described it as "an honor and credit to the people of Skyberg." That same year the Farmers' Elevator Company organized, with F. J. White its manager. Successive improvements included a new depot, sidewalks along the one business street, a meat market, a second hardware store, and a traveling library. Some of these were short-lived, but they suggest a degree of prosperity not enjoyed by most rural villages of that time. Still, frequent changes in the ownership of some of the business places hint of a struggle to make satisfactory profit.

By the middle of the second decade of the 20th century, some of the bloom was off Skyberg's prosperity. Private parties had run the so-called farmers' elevator for some years, and some business places had closed their doors. Then, in 1915, the town entered upon a second boom period. The chief motive force was a bank proposed by a group of Minneapolis men. The Farmers State Bank of Skyberg, authorized on August 21 and open for business two days later, brought an illusion of prosperity. Immediately there were predictions of a hardware store, a butcher shop, and a lumberyard—all of which came to fruition the next year. In October the *Leader*'s Skyberg correspondent reported that several families wanted to move to the village but could find no houses. "Who says Skyberg is dead?" he asked. "Every hitching post was in service and the sidewalks crowded with people all day Monday and Wednesday."

The prosperity was real enough for a time, but when the state bank examiner closed the bank in February 1919, Skyberg received a shock from which it never fully recovered. The speculations of the nonresident members of the board of directors were the cause of the bank's failure. A new bank, locally owned and organized, opened for business in the spring of 1920, but Skyberg's great day was over. By 1926, when a candidate for county school superintendent toured the countryside in search of votes and published his discoveries as "Little Visits" in local newspapers, only six business places still functioned. The six included two general stores (one about to close), a hardware store, the bank, the creamery, and one elevator, which also sold coal from the sheds of the "old lumber company."

Francis J. White sold his store late in 1922 to Joe Corrigan, a former Skyberg resident who had been living for some years in North Dakota. On February 10, 1923, Mrs. Vera R. Corrigan became acting postmaster. On April 25 her appointment was made permanent. Subsequently the post office passed into the hands of Nels Fennie, who had taken over the former hardware store to run as a grocery store. He became acting postmaster December 6, 1930, confirmed November 7, 1931.

By that time a major disaster had befallen Skyberg. In 1928, the state securities commission denied a request to remove the bank to West Concord. In 1930 as the Great Depression settled over the nation, the proposal was renewed, this time with success. The bank closed that summer, its assets sold to the Farmers' State Bank of West Concord. The newspapers stated the reason—there was no longer enough business to warrant a bank in Skyberg.

From that time forward, Skyberg declined. In 1931 the CGW railroad substituted custodian service for agency service (see page 28) at "Skyburg." Before another decade passed, the grain elevator went out of business; eventually it was torn down. Andrew Monson bought the White store building upon construction of T.H. 56 in 1938 and moved it to his farm. Later it was returned to Skyberg, where a man named Overby used some sections to build a new store. Overby also bought the old hall building from the Modern Woodmen of America, but it burned just after the its residents moved out. After the Meyer store closed in 1926, two parties successively used it as a tavern. In 1947 the Skyberg Cooperative Creamery Association, after a steady loss of business, dissolved.

Creamery at Skyberg. *GCHS*

The postal history of Skyberg is of a piece with the decline of the village. In 1943 the rural route operating from the post office came to an end. A Kenyon route was extended to serve the Skyberg patrons. The post office changed hands twice more in its last years. On March 29, 1948, the new proprietor of the Fennie store, Chester B. Swanson, became postmaster. He served only until January 1, when Evald E. Erickson replaced him. The final blow came in 1951, when one of the two remaining business places in Skyberg, the Erickson store, closed along with the post office. The proposal to close the office came up during the summer, at which time the patrons petitioned the Post Office Department to postpone action until investigation could be made. Through the efforts of Congressman August H. Andresen, the department ordered a delay. But on November 30 the Skyberg post office was discontinued.

Not much remains of Skyberg today. With both the elevator and the depot gone, there is no evidence of a town where the rail once ran. The railroad, once the main line of the CGW, was abandoned in 1981, its tracks taken up two years later. The old Fennie store was razed a few years after it closed. The other store, operated last by the Lundberg family, closed in the early 1960s and was torn down in 1966. In its last years it operated more or less on demand—there was insufficient trade to keep it open. The original Skyberg store, used for many years as a residence, was torn down a few months earlier. The bank building remained for a few years longer, deteriorating a little each year. In the summer of 1972 West Concord's volunteer fire department burned it. With only six houses left in the community, little remains of Skyberg to merit the label *ghost town*. Not even a highway sign identifies it.

Sogn
Named for a district in Norway and located in section 24 of Warsaw, Sogn was a latecomer among Goodhue County post offices. Not established until May 18, 1892, it lasted little more than a decade. Contemporary newspaper references suggest that there were no business places in the immediate vicinity at the time the office opened. The gazetteers do not list Ola A. Tveitmoe, the first postmaster, as proprietor of a store served by any post office in the area. A few months earlier the *Cannon Falls Beacon* reported that Severt Jellum (usually *Gjellum*) was agitating to have the Wangs post office moved three miles east. Soon thereafter he apparently tried to have the milk separator moved. Early in April the paper reported that the separator was in section 24. The Crystal Creamery Company of Kenyon, which had set up several such countryside enterprises, owned the separator. By August 1893 local farmers were meeting to discuss buying it or building one of their own.

Whether or not Sogn had a store in 1892, it did have one late the following year. By August 1893, Abel P. Brandvold, "the Sogn merchant," was building a store, and in November, John O. Underdahl became his partner in the mercantile business, apparently in operation by that time. About a year later, Underdahl sold his interest in the store to R. P. Brandvold, and the firm became Brandvold Brothers. Contemporary records mention no addition to the commercial life of the community over the next several years. Some sentiment emerged for promoting a town there as early as 1892, when rumor had it that Sogn would be platted into lots and blocks. "The Sognese [*sic*] are bent on building a city there," reported the *Beacon*.

Tveitmoe did not long remain postmaster. Active in the Populist Party, he soon went to Crookston to edit a Populist newspaper. Newspapers referred to A. P. Brandvold, Tveitmoe's replacement on October 23, 1893, more than two

Sogn store. *GCHS*

months before that date. Brandvold continued as postmaster until October 19, 1897, when Marcus Charlson, who with his brother Jonas had taken over the store, succeeded him. By this time Sogn, according to the gazetteer for 1898–99, had, in addition to the store and the creamery, two carpenters, a painter and paperhanger, two produce firms, a shoemaker, a wagonmaker, and a blacksmith. The roster was much the same in 1900 except that the shoemaker was also running a hotel and a cheese factory—the Sogn Cooperative Dairy Asso-

Cobbler Peder Fretheim in Sogn. Behind him at right is the store. *GCHS*

ciation, organized in December of the previous year—had replaced the privately operated milk separator. The first manager of the cheese factory was A. T. Jones, who held the job intermittently for several years.

This period marked the high point of Sogn's history. Sogn was never platted, though a news item in 1913 might have led the unwary to suppose it had metropolitan ambitions. Announcement of a Fourth of July celebration indicated a chance to buy lots in the "newly-platted city of Sogn." The St. Paul Southern Electric Railway was building towards Sogn, it said, and cars would be running in a year's time. A consolidated school, opera house, and hall supposedly were planned. Evidently the item was a burlesque of the extravagant town-promotion schemes reflected in many weekly newspapers of the time.

With the coming of RFD, the Sogn post office went the way of the rest. On January 31, 1903, it closed. Mail for its patrons went to Dennison. In the spring of 1904 the Charlson brothers, together with Sogn resident John H. Otterness, started a store in the new town of Bombay. They did not dispose of their holdings at Sogn, however, until 1906, when they sold out to Lars Lillesve. At the time they apparently managed the cheese factory as well as the store.

The Sogn store and cheese factory continued in business for many years. Ted Stenhaug operated the store for some time, followed by Ernest L. Swanson, William Blagsvedt, Irv C. Crotten, and Guy Barsness. Rudolph Charlson opened a Conoco filling station at Sogn in 1934. The cheese factory building having outlived its usefulness, the Sogn co-op in 1941 constructed a modern

The Sogn store, 1953. *RWM*

brick plant, just in time for the economic crisis that caused many rural cream-eries and cheese factories to close their doors. In an attempt to keep their factory going, the farmers rented it to John Roch of Pine Island and later to Arco Dairies. Beginning about 1956 they turned to selling whole milk to the Webster Dairy Co-op, but even this solution proved temporary. By February 1, 1959, the Sogn factory was closed. Just six months later, the store went out of business. The building was later remodeled as a dwelling, its false front removed. After 1959 the only business place remaining in the village on the Little Cannon was the filling station. Adolph Stenhaug operated it after 1944 and closed it in 1987. Banker's Honey used the former cheese factory for the storage of bee-keeping equipment for a time. That and a clus-ter of eight houses at the junction of Goodhue County Highways 9 and 14 make up the hamlet of Sogn today.

Spencer

Early in the history of Vasa township, settlers saw possibilities for a town at the point where the Red Wing-to-Faribault road crossed Belle Creek. Three mill sites in the southeast quarter of section 4 led to the survey of part of this tract in April 1856. The plat, recorded on January 9, 1857, shows 15 streets and 35 numbered blocks—in short, a paper city—complete with "Public Grounds" and three irregular tracts labeled "mill property."

The Spencer post office opened October 4, 1856, with postmaster Hans Mattson, who later enjoyed a career in public affairs. Phineas S. Fish, who appears as proprietor of the plat of Spencer, succeeded Mattson on April 23, 1857. Fish remained postmaster until June 27, 1860, when Sven P. Petterson assumed the office. Gustefnus Peterson (February 27, 1865), Charles Johnson (July 26,1865), Andrew C. Hillberg (June 26, 1866), and John Paulson (Octo-ber 7, 1867) followed. On October 14, 1868, the name was changed to Vasa, with no change of postmaster.

Since Spencer was the predecessor of the Vasa post office, the question arises as to when the office moved to Vasa village. Mattson's claim, recorded in May 1856, lay in section 15, where the village later grew up. The office prob-ably was there for the few months Mattson was postmaster. During Fish's three years, the office probably was on his claim in section 4, where Spencer was platted. All Fish's successors have Swedish names, and they may have kept the office elsewhere than the townsite, which never developed much beyond pa-per. One tradition holds that the office for a time operated from somewhere along what is now the Vasa-Welch road, in section 34, township 113. John Paulson, during whose term the name was changed, at that time managed the "Vasa Farmers' Union Store," organized in 1868 at the village. The Spencer post office probably was at Vasa before the official change of name. Spencer village had slipped into oblivion well before that event.

Spring Creek

One of the most completely rural post offices in the county was Spring Creek, in Cherry Grove township. As nearly as can be determined, it operated during most of its 42 years from farmhouses, moving from place to place with changes of postmaster.

Spring Creek opened May 12, 1860, with Leonard Briggs postmaster. A native of Massachusetts, then 63, he had lived in New York before coming to Minnesota. In March 1858 he filed a claim in the southwest quarter of section 5, presumably the first post office site. A small stream flowing just east of his land provided its name. Samuel L. Brown succeeded Briggs on December 15, 1864, holding the office about six months until Harvey F. Billings replaced him on July 11, 1865. Billings gave way on December 30, 1865, to Beriah C. Wait. He was postmaster nearly eight years until Walter B. Wait took over on July 11, 1873. Decennial census schedules provide the only readily accessible information about these men. Billings and his brother Henry (see below), born in Pennsylvania, had come to Minnesota in the first years of settlement, becoming substantial farmers in their new homes. Harvey was 33 in 1870, Henry 44. The Waits were father and son, ages 46 and 17, both born in New York. Nothing else is known of these early postmasters, and Spring Creek is not listed in gazetteers of the time. The only specific fact about the office appears in a report to the Post Office Department in 1870—its location in the southwest corner of section 4.

Two brief postmaster appointments followed the second Wait. On November 11, 1874, Henry M. Billings became postmaster. Jens Bugge followed on March 1, 1876. The next postmaster, Jacob O. Strandness, had a longer term. Appointed June 7, 1877, he held the office until Duane S. Root replaced him on February 19, 1886. Strandness, born in Norway about 1845, ran a small store in the northeast corner of section 5, near the junction of the present T.H. 60 and Goodhue County Highway 1, a mile east of Bombay. In 1877 a blacksmith shop operated from just across the road in Wanamingo township. Strandness's successor, Root, had a farm in the northeast part of section 8, a mile south of where Strandness had lived. He was the son of Byington Root, one of the early settlers of Cherry Grove township, whose frequent moves followed a familiar pattern. Born in Connecticut, he had lived for varying periods in Ohio, New York, and Wisconsin before settling in Minnesota. The last postmaster at Spring Creek, John H. Bradley, started October 11, 1886. His farm, on the southwest quarter of section 9, was the site of the post office until it closed on September 30, 1902. A blacksmith shop reportedly operated there about 1893.

A Spring Creek column appeared for years in the *Kenyon Leader*, even after the post office closed, without reference to any business place there. Spring Creek seems to have been a rural neighborhood, covering a wide area, rather than a village or hamlet. When the Milwaukee branch line from Faribault to Zumbrota was built in 1903, there was some local sentiment for naming the

Bombay station *Spring Creek*. The railroad paid no heed, and the name, except as applied to the tributary of the Zumbro, was forgotten.

Stanton
Stanton is one of several towns established at one place, then moved to another after the railroad bypassed the original site. Many of the earliest white settlers in Stanton township were of New England origin, and several bore the surname Stanton. In January 1857 William and John Stanton, six other men, and one woman hired H. H. Benson to survey a square mile in sections 29 and 32 and plat it into blocks and streets. They registered the town plat at the Goodhue County Register of Deeds office on February 25, 1857. A sizable townsite, it contained 72 blocks, seven east-west streets, and seven north-south streets. It centered where today's Minnesota T.H. 19, approaching from the west, meets T.H. 56. Centre Street is today's T.H. 56, and Cannon Street is T.H. 19 and its eastward extension, 330th Street.[7] Probably no other streets were laid out on the ground because, according to a plat note on file in the county recorder's office, most of it was vacated on May 21, 1864.

Vacation of the plat of "old" Stanton did not mean the end of the community. The 1877 Warner & Foote county map shows a mill, blacksmith shop, rural school, Methodist Episcopal Church, and cemetery, all within bounds of the former plat. The mill, situated on Prairie Creek, is of special interest because it escaped mention in county histories as well as in contemporary Cannon Falls newspapers. The 1877 map gives the owner of the land surrounding the mill as E. S. Bailey. Surely this is the Bailey associated with the early history of the Granville mills, which later developed into Cascade. The Stanton mill probably had a short career. Whatever the case in the 1870s, the flow of Prairie Creek today is insufficient to power a mill. Even then, its current across the nearly level Stanton Flats must have been sluggish at best.

Old Stanton had a post office during the entire period preceding its removal to the later railroad station. The Stanton post office opened on October 14, 1857, and William Stanton, whose name heads the list of the town's proprietors, was postmaster. John Thomas succeeded him on August 7, 1861. On August 23, 1862, Edmund S. Bailey, presumably the owner of the mill, took it over. Samuel B. Vinton became postmaster on December 10, 1866, and John Stanton followed on September 17, 1869. Carrie Bailey was next, starting April 17, 1873. William Goudy, appointed on November 15, 1873, was the last postmaster to serve old Stanton. He retained the office for more than ten years. His name appears on the 1877 map as the owner of a small tract across the road from the blacksmith shop. Although the map mentions no store, Goudy (described as a farmer in 1860) appears in the 1870 census as a "retail grocer."

The service afforded the Stanton post office was not altogether satisfactory. In 1878 Congress established a post route from Northfield to Holden via Wangs and Stanton. Some five years later, when a new route opened from Cannon Falls to Wastedo, the *Beacon* commented: "The next thing is a route between here and Stanton as the people in that vicinity are but little better off than those of Wastedo." Apparently no change occurred. By that time other developments were in the works; old Stanton was about to receive its death blow.

The construction in 1885 of the Minnesota and Northwestern line, which formed the nucleus of the later CGW, killed old Stanton and brought into being the village a half-mile west. This was the brainchild of Alpheus Beede Stickney, who earlier had worked for James J. Hill on what became the Great Northern and who had built the Minnesota Central (Cannon Valley) railroad in 1882. The arrival of the M&NW led to the demise of Cascade, to the establishment of Randolph, Dennison, and Nerstrand, and to the expansion of Kenyon.

Through 1884 there were rumors of the imminent construction of the new railroad. On December 5 the *Beacon* reported that the citizens of western Stanton township were sending round a petition asking the M&NW for a depot. The laying of track began the next spring and proceeded from Cascade, where rails had been stored over the winter. At the nearest point the new railroad passed little more than a half-mile west of old Stanton. According to postal records of September 26, 1885, the post office was 205 rods (3,382 feet) east of the proposed railway station. This placed it just about where an 1877 map shows William Goudy's property.

The removal of the post office to the railroad station is precisely datable. On February 19, 1886, Mary M. Dack became postmaster; she was reappointed on March 11. John and Mary Dack owned the land where the railway station stood, and when "new" Stanton was platted a decade later, the Dacks were its proprietors. Mary Dack did not remain postmaster for long. In the spring of 1887 the *Beacon* reported her resignation, and Andrew A. Beaurline ("a first-class man") replaced her. Beaurline, who started April 26, 1887, had served twice as postmaster at Wastedo. Probably he operated a store there and did so again in the new railroad town.

Beaurline remained postmaster until 1892, when, on March 31, George C. Leyh (as listed on the appointment register in the National Archives) replaced him. During the eight years Leyh served as postmaster, the new town of Stanton developed into a trading center of some importance. It had made considerable progress by 1894. The Foote & Henion county atlas published that year shows a general store/post office, a blacksmith shop, two "warehouses" (probably grain elevators)—one on either side of the depot—stockyards, and *two* creameries. Along the railroad was the Crescent Creamery, and just north of the later Nelson hotel building (still standing in 2000) was the Stanton Creamery and Cheese Factory.

In the early days of white settlement the practice was to lay out a plat and hope a town would develop. By the 1880s town promoters had adopted a more realistic course of action: wait to see whether a town developed, then plat it. John and Mary Dack platted new Stanton on April 26, 1895, though they did not file the plat with the Register of Deeds until September 16, 1897. This Stanton, confined to a strip of land on the west side of the railroad track, was modest compared with the original townsite. It included most of the business places then existing. There were not many houses in Stanton at that time.

The post office changed hands on April 13, 1900, when John Amundson became postmaster. Henry W. Nelson succeeded Amundson on November 3, 1906. He and his son, Virgil W. Nelson, served successively for most of the Stanton post office's remaining 75 years. In 1906, the elder Nelson built a hotel, in which he also kept a general store and post office. The strategically located hotel attracted passengers from the trains passing through Stanton daily during the early 20th century. The route became the main line of the CGW from the Twin Cities to both Kansas City and Chicago.

A decade later, during the 1915–16 wave of bank startups in small towns, Stanton, like Frontenac, Skyberg, Welch, and White Rock, added a bank to its roster. Authorized on April 1, 1916, with capital and surplus of $12,000, the State Bank of Stanton was promoted mainly by nonresidents. W. W. Pye of Northfield was president, A. O. Lenzinger of Webster vice president, and J. F. Lenzinger cashier. As cashier, the latter Lenzinger at least was obliged to live in Stanton while on the job. By the end of the fiscal year on June 30 the bank reported resources of $28,417.96.

For the first three decades of the 20th century, Stanton prospered, perhaps reaching its peak about the mid-1920s. A 1924 gazetteer lists an array of businesses there. Besides the Nelson general store, there was another grocery, run by Joseph Johnson. The village also boasted a grain elevator owned by the Commander Elevator Company and managed by F. A. Strom. There was a cheese factory run by the Twin Cities Milk Producers Association, Harry Hysell manager; the State Bank of Stanton, R. W. Pye president, Harlan Pye cashier (a 1933 advertisement used the pi symbol for the Pyes' bank); a garage owned by Arthur H. and Robert J. Swarts; and the billiard parlor of Vincent J. Kukacka, plus a blacksmith shop run by William McCorkell and a feed business operated by Amos W. Swinton. George Burch managed the stockyards owned by the Live Stock Shippers Association, and Louis A. Tolstad served as depot agent. A rural school and a Methodist church, successor to the one built in 1874, rounded out the entries for Stanton, credited with a population of 100.

Like most other small communities, Stanton declined during the Great Depression. The bank closed its doors sometime during this period. As late as 1936, however, a county map prepared by the Minnesota Highway Department showed the creamery and five other business places still in operation—and 21 houses. In the next half-century all the businesses closed. In the 1950s Virgil

Nelson, who succeeded his father as postmaster on August 12, 1939, and his wife, Elaine, began developing an Old Country Store, as a sort of adjunct to the general store he had inherited. Intended as a tourist attraction, the collection included items such as buttonhooks, stone canning jars, a brass cuspidor, bins for spices, flour, and sugar, lamp chimneys, old furniture, and stove polish. The original Henry Nelson general store supplied the nucleus of this assemblage, but the son hunted for items not found there and built up an impressive stock of what might have been found in a general store of the very early 20th century. A May 1957 article in the *Red Wing Republican Eagle* includes photos of part of this stock.

If the effort to recapture the mood of a bygone era suggested a certain nostalgia, it also reflected the obsolescence of villages like Stanton as well as the country post office. By 1957 the days of Stanton's post office were numbered, though it survived another 24 years. It closed on July 31, 1981. Since then the people of Stanton have received their mail by rural carrier from Dennison. Although correspondence about its possible reopening as a community post office continued another four years, the closing was final.

The Stanton of 2000 had as many houses as appeared on the 1936 map, but there were no businesses. The Stanton Methodist Church thrived, and the township hall was still in the village. The Nelson hotel/store stands, part of it rented for apartments. But today's town is only a ghost of the busy settlement of 1924. Motorists on T.H. 19 are invited to slow to 45 mph as they pass through Stanton (a demand not made of those passing through Hader on U.S. 52), and a highway sign identifies the town. Although there are two houses in Old Stanton, neither dates from the time the community flourished.

Sunapee
Predecessor to Roscoe Centre, the Sunapee post office opened on August 5, 1858. Truman Parker, later postmaster at Poplar Grove, was postmaster. Charles Parker followed on December 1, 1859, serving until the name change on August 12, 1863. The Parkers may have been related, but the 1860 census gives Truman's birthplace as New York and Charles's (five years older) as Connecticut. Charles Parker lived for several years in Ohio before coming to Minnesota.

Truman Parker made a claim in October 1860 to part of the southwest quarter of section 14. If he resided there upon establishment of the post office, its first location was about two-and-a-half miles southeast of the present hamlet of Roscoe Center. The change of name accompanied by a change in postmaster suggests that the office was moved at that time. An item in the *Goodhue County Republican* also indicates a site change. It states that the post office at Sunapee had closed, with a new one called Roscoe Centre established between Zumbrota and Roscoe. Sunapee is the name of a lake in New Hampshire. Probably an early settler suggested the name to commemorate his former home. A proposal to name the township *Sunapee* was rejected in favor of *Roscoe*.

Thoten
On March 18, 1878, the name of the recently established Belvidere post office was changed to Thoten. Anthon N. Jenson, first postmaster at Belvidere, remained in the position until June 21, 1880, when John C. Johnson succeeded him. John A. Larson succeeded Johnson on July 10, 1882, and Johnson returned March 26, 1883. The following July 23 the office closed with further mail sent to Belle Chester.

The Thoten post office served a Norwegian community (as the name suggests) in the central and southwestern parts of Belvidere township. The location probably shifted with the changes in postmaster. Jenson appears in the 1880 census as a merchant. On the south line of section 16, where the Belvidere town hall now stands, there was once a store, probably Jenson's. If so, it may have been the original location of the Thoten post office. Johnson's farm was in the southwest quarter of section 16, and Larson's was a mile west. The post office no doubt occupied each of these sites. Between the two was a Norwegian Methodist church built in 1874. Only a weed-grown cemetery remains.

Vasa
As noted earlier, a group of Vasa township farmers, aiming to secure the advantages of cooperative merchandising, in 1868 organized the "Vasa Farmers' Union." The union shortly erected a store east of the Lutheran church near the center of the township. John Paulson, secretary of the company, was manager. He also opened a hotel in connection with the store. Appointed postmaster in 1867 at what was then the Spencer post office, he retained the position after the name change. Not until November 11, 1870, did John G. Gustafson replace him as postmaster. Gustafson's term of office was brief, for Lewis Engberg took over on December 29 that year. According to the Wood & Alley county history (1878), Engberg and John Norelius formed a partnership in a general store in 1871. This lasted until 1877, when, on June 20, Norelius sold his interest to Charles J. Johnson and built the Vasa House, a hotel.

How much of a settlement existed before establishment of the farmers' store is unclear, but in the following years a business center grew there. The decennial census lists several nonfarmers in Vasa township, including an extraordinary number of blacksmiths. Since the census usually does not list post office addresses, determining which of these business and professional men lived at Vasa village and which at White Rock is difficult. An 1872 state gazetteer lists a store, three churches, and a hotel. One issued six years later added a milling firm, a blacksmith, a painter and paperhanger, a physician, and a music teacher.

Ofelt store, formerly the Engberg store and post office, Vasa. *GCHS*

The mill appears on the 1877 Warner & Foote map and may have been in existence for some time before that. It was on Belle Creek, about a mile and a half west of the village, in the south half of the southwest quarter of the northwest quarter of section 16. When S. S. Lewis, editor of the *Cannon Falls Beacon*, made a trip to Vasa in August 1882, he stopped at the mill, then (as in 1877) operated by Solomon Nelson. According to Lewis, Nelson's mill did a large custom business at that time. Lewis was especially interested in a mineral spring on the property, which Nelson and Dr. John H. Sandberg were planning to improve with some new buildings for the benefit of visitors—presumably including a hotel. No further mention of the project appeared in the *Beacon*. Nelson supposedly drowned in July 1888, trying to save a man who fell into Belle Creek while working on a bridge west of the village. Whether the mill ceased operation after his death is unknown. The 1880 census lists another miller, bearing the undistinguished name of John Johnson. Since there is no evidence of a second mill, he probably was associated with Nelson at the mill on Belle Creek.

In 1877 the citizens built a town hall (which still stands), and in 1898 a cooperative creamery was organized there. The unused Baptist church became a creamery, serving in that capacity until 1916, when it burned. A modern brick-and-tile building replaced it. After many successful years, the creamery fell on hard times after World War II and endured increasing pressure to consolidate with a larger concern. It finally went out of business about 1972. A garage and filling station that long served the community also gave up the ghost.

Vasa remained a thriving village, centered on the Swedish Lutheran Church and its auxiliary institutions, until well into the 20th century. Not all the Vasa residents were Lutherans. The community at one time also supported Baptist and Methodist churches. The Baptist church, whose membership included such early businessmen as Charles Johnson and John Norelius, lasted only a few decades, but the Methodist church survived into the 20th century as well. Services were discontinued in 1939 but resumed in 1946, only to end for good in 1951. The Bartlett family bought the church building, built in 1866, and moved it to the northwest quarter of the northwest quarter of section 6 in Goodhue township.

Lewis Engberg had held the Vasa postmastership until September 16, 1885, when he was succeeded by Hans L. Brynhildsen, who served as postmaster until October 29, 1897. After these relatively long incumbencies, the office changed hands more frequently in the next few years. Ferdinand L. Engeberg, Brynildsen's successor, held it only until August 25 of the following year, when Nels C. Eklund (or Ecklund) replaced him. Eklund remained postmaster for more than six years, then sold his store late in 1904 to Nathan B. Ofelt, who took over as postmaster on June 27, 1905.

Unlike all the other Goodhue County post offices located off the railroads, Vasa did not succumb to RFD. Larger than any other "inland" town, the village was apparently considered sufficiently important to merit retaining its post office. After serving as postmaster nearly 12 years, Ofelt was replaced on

The Ofelt store became the Julian store and post office, above in 1952. *RWM*

Akerson store at Vasa, 1940. *RWM*

March 17, 1917, by Clarence A. Julian, who had come to Vasa two years earlier and gone into the general merchandise business. The post office, which had
been moved back and forth between the two general stores, remained in the
Julian store for the rest of its existence. When Julian died, August 26, 1955, his
widow closed the store, and on October 31 of that year the Vasa post office
closed. Postal service in the village was retained a few months longer, however,
for on November 1 a rural station tributary to the Welch post office opened in
the other store, operated until his death in 1952 by Rudolph P. Akerson.[8] But
the tributary closed along with the store on May 31, 1956. Vasa, which until
1955 had supported two stores, has since 1956 supported none.

     Although there are still about 25 houses in Vasa, the village no longer
boasts any business places. When rural schools gave way to consolidation, the
people of Vasa built a new school, similar to one built near Wastedo. But after
a few years it, too, closed its doors and joined a larger district. The building was
taken over by the Vasa Lutheran church, which remains the one vital institution
in the village. A museum testifies to the community's interest in its history. One
of the major centers of Swedish settlement in Minnesota, Vasa lives on, no
longer a trading center but still a community proud of its heritage.

Wacouta

A rival of Red Wing in the county seat election of 1853, Wacouta was the second community in Goodhue County to open a post office. Besides the abortive

"Wah-coo-ta" office, which later became Red Wing, two later offices bore this name, with slightly different spellings and locations.

On September 28, 1854, James B. Smith became postmaster at Wacoota, a prospective city at the head of Lake Pepin. George W. Bullard and Abner W. Post had settled there in 1850. Bullard was licensed to trade with the Indians, but much of his business came from the lumbermen congregated across the river in Wisconsin. Post built a house for Bullard, and the two started a sawmill. Several other settlers followed in 1852 and 1853, and in 1854 Smith built a hotel. The next year Daniel Saunders erected another. In April 1855 Bullard had a tract of land surveyed into lots and blocks. This plat, recorded on June 21 as the village of Wacoota, occupied portions of section 36, range 14, and section 31, range 13, in Wacouta township, along the lakeshore. Meridian Street marked the section line. Including additions made in 1856 and 1858, the plat contained 83 blocks, many of them fractional and irregular in shape.

The original Wacoota did not develop into the metropolis its promoters expected, but it survived and retained a post office for 15 years. George Post succeeded Smith as postmaster on October 20, 1855. Bullard replaced him on April 22, 1857. After about three years in the office, on April 20, 1860, Elizabeth Post Bullard succeeded him. She remained postmaster until the Wacoota post office closed on September 20, 1869. The Mitchell history remarks that in 1857 the postmaster's commissions amounted to $75 a quarter. By 1869, the year of publication, they were down to about $5 a year.

The original town of Wacoota, with its three hotels (Bullard had built a large one in 1857) and its county-seat aspirations, was by this time practically abandoned. Not until 1889, however, was any part of the plat—that west of Meridian Street—vacated. Four years later Wacoota was replatted on a more modest scale, chiefly as a site for the summer residences of Red Wing people. This development has continued ever since.

Meanwhile, the county's first railroad was built in 1870 with a station located about three-quarters of a mile inland from the old town. The next year O. Eames, later a cooper in Red Wing, was running a store at Wacouta. Whether this was on the lake or at the station is unclear. In 1874, however, a post office opened at the station, and Caroline Phares Bullard Drum became postmaster on September 25. The name was now spelled *Wacouta* to conform with that of the township. Drum was the widow of George W. Bullard, who had died in 1863.

The new Wacouta post office operated for nearly 30 years and at different times occupied at least two sites, less than a half-mile apart, on the north side of what is now U.S. 61. Drum served as postmaster until May 2, 1889, when Etta M. Thurber replaced her. May R. S. Post followed Thurber on May 7, 1890, lasting only until November 7, when Elizabeth Church took the job. After a little more than five years, Peter Martin became postmaster, on December 3, 1895. Elizabeth Church took over again on August 25, 1899.

On March 5, 1904, the Wacouta post office closed, another casualty of RFD.

Small as it is, Wacouta township was the location of another now vanished community, Sevastopol, sometimes confused with Wacouta proper. Intended primarily for the convenience of lumbermen floating rafts down the Mississippi, Sevastopol, chiefly a collection of taverns, had few of the attributes of a permanent settlement and no post office. Yet it was platted in July 1857 under the proprietorship of John H. Elder, Hugh Adams, and G. I. Richards, none apparently residing in the county. The plat was recorded August 22, 1857.

Located in section 26, about a mile and a half above old Wacoota, Sevastopol consisted of 23 blocks, plus a "Church Block" and a "School Block." Unlike Wacoota, laid out on mostly level terrain, Sevastopol occupied a hollow at the mouth of a narrow coulee, surrounded by steep bluffs. Had the place prospered, it would have had no room for expansion. As it was, Sevastopol remained largely a paper city. According to C. A. Rasmussen, many lots were sold, but changes in the lumber business left the embryo town without a reason for existence. The village was soon abandoned, its plat never vacated.

No one has positively determined the origin of the Sevastopol name. One legend has it that some of the town's founders were present at the siege of Sevastopol in the Crimean War and named it because of a fancied resemblance to that Russian city. More likely, someone who saw the stage play *The Siege of Sevastopol* chose the name.

Though Sevastopol has vanished, Wacouta survives as a kind of suburb of Red Wing. Besides many houses and summer cottages near the site of the original town, there is a former store building erected along the highway and railroad track in 1926 by Fred A. Scherf and his wife, Ernestine. After his death in the early 1930s, she ran the store another two years or so as the Orange Jug. There she sold Red Wing pottery, glassware, antiques, and candy. After further changes of ownership, the store was acquired in the mid-1940s by Edward and Dora Saville, succeeded by Raleigh and Myrtle Albrecht. The Albrechts, who had lived in Japan, remodeled the building with an Oriental look and sold Japanese artifacts. For a time the building also served as a motel. The owners in 1999 were Norman and Nancy Berger. They sold Western wear, saddles, gift items, and antiques.

The Dutch Oven restaurant, built by Edward Saupe near the Wacouta store in 1928, served many years as an unofficial community center. After Saupe's death in 1948, his sons ran it for several years, then finally closed it. The building was demolished in the late 1960s.

With the Wacouta school closed in the early 1950s, the only building of an institutional nature is the town hall, a half-mile inland from the store. Not far away is the Wacouta cemetery, bearing the name on its gate and thus identifying the community. A short street in downtown St. Paul—Wacouta—commemorates the village.

Wangs

Long after the short-lived Miami post office had expired and Norwegian immigrants populated Warsaw township, a post office named Wangs opened near its center. Even J. Evenson became its first postmaster on June 5, 1876. Evenson, like all but three of his 13 successors, bore a Norwegian name. (One of the three exceptions bore an anglicized Norwegian name.) During the Wangs post office's 25 years, only one postmaster—the last—served for as much as four years. Several held the job less than a year.

Evenson served only nine months, unless we suppose his successor, Even J. Tvedt, appointed March 2, 1877, was one and the same, no longer using the Scandinavian patronymic. In any case, on November 6, 1877, Tosten A. Melhouse became postmaster, apparently in an acting capacity, for he was reappointed on December 11. Melhouse, or Melhuus, as the name appears in the county histories, was at that time 33 years old. The previous July he had opened a store at Wangs in partnership with Botolf O. Flesche.

The firm of Melhuus & Flesche did not last long, for by 1880 Brusegaard & Olson were running the Wangs store. Thomas Brusegaard served a brief term as postmaster, succeeding George E. Sheets, appointed August 4, 1879. Brusegaard served from August 9, 1880, to November 23, when Albert E. Sheets replaced him. By then Wangs boasted, in addition to the store, a blacksmith shop run by Charles J. Bjerva (Christian Bjerva in the 1880 census), and a boot-and-shoe concern operated by P. T. Kulaas. The 1880 gazetteer

The Wangs store in 1940. *RWM*

listed T. P. Kulaas (perhaps related to P. T. Kulaas) and A. A. Lee as carpenters. Two years later George Sheets had taken over the store, and "G. Western & Company" had started another store. Western, who lived in Cannon Falls, left the management of the store to Albert Sheets.

During the decade of the 1880s Wangs experienced a bewildering turnover in postmasters, not due entirely to changes in ownership of the stores. Carl N. Lien started March 27, 1882. Thomas J. Austin succeeded him on July 3. Lien was back by November 19, 1883, but Knut M. Myhre replaced him on June 27, 1884. Lien returned again on December 27, 1886. Myhre was the partner of J. A. Kolstad, who ran the principal store for many years after Myhre left the business. Kolstad's widow operated it with the aid of her children until her death in 1946. The Kolstads' daughter Selma remembered her father as post-master, but the records of the Post Office Department do not give his name. Still, nearly everyone else in the community had a crack at the job at one time or another.

Nils L. Nesheim became postmaster on December 5, 1890. Ludwig M. Hamery succeeded him on July 13, 1892. Gertrude Hoverstad started June 23, 1893, serving less than a month, until July 19, when Nels O. Gaasedalen took the job. Before the year was out, Wangs had still another postmaster, Christopher T. Strand, appointed October 14. He served for the office's remaining eight years. Strand, probably like other postmasters, was for a time proprietor of the second store in the hamlet. This store, built in 1893, operated for a time under the firm name of Strand & Skeen. By 1900 it was in the hands of Brekke Brothers. Strand remained postmaster.

Wangs still had several business places during this period. Besides the two stores, the blacksmith shop and shoe shop continued, though under changing management. A creamery had started in 1893 or shortly afterward to replace the milk separator that moved to Sogn. Listed in a 1900 gazetteer with owner B. O. Brekke, it must have gone out of business a few years later, for by 1904 T. Stenhaug had bought the building with the intention of moving it to his farm and converting it to a tenant house.

By the turn of the century, conditions were no longer favorable to the survival of rural trading centers like Wangs. The closing of the post office on August 31, 1901, was only one indication of the gradual decline and virtual disappearance of the hamlet. One by one the business places closed their doors and were torn down, until only the Kolstad store remained. Upon Mrs. Mary Kolstad's death in 1946, the store temporarily closed—after 63 years of continuous operation, reported the *Kenyon Leader*. The next year Clarence and Helen Nesseth remodeled and reopened it. The Nesseths ran the store until August 1954, selling it to Joseph and Mildred Marko. After continuing the business for nearly five years, the Markos closed the store on April 1, 1959, and remodeled it for a dwelling. Thus occurred the last gasp of business activity in Wangs in the same year the store and cheese factory closed at Sogn, two-and-a-half miles away.

Wastedo
As noted previously, three villages—Hader, Roscoe, and Wastedo—had closely parallel histories. All three were "paper cities," but all developed somewhat beyond the paper stage. Goodhue County's first published history oversimplified and exaggerated the situation a dozen years after Wastedo's founding, when it recorded that Henry K. Terrell, the town's proprietor, had taken

> an even section of land, and had it surveyed and laid out into town lots, and a paper city was the result, which was christened Wastedo, with churches, school houses and business blocks, *ad libitum*, but all these brilliant schemes proved to be but castles *de Espagne*, as the real city never reached a greater growth than one house. As the city refused to grow in accordance with the anticipations of the proprietors, the plat was vacated and made into farms.

The facts are slightly less dramatic. Terrell had the east half of section 21, Leon township, surveyed in July 1857 and laid out into lots, blocks, and streets.[9] The project was more ambitious than in Roscoe, less so than in Hader. The plat included 98 blocks, including outlots, and the customary public square. The only justification for the establishment of a town here was that the new route of the St. Paul and Dubuque stage line ran through it. There was no stream to furnish waterpower for a mill and no other inducement. Yet Terrell thought a town could be viable. His confederate, Edwin A. Sargent, opened a store that summer and got himself appointed postmaster on September 26. Streets named Terrell and Sargent, shown directly across the public square from one another, indicate the two were allies. Other platted streets honored Washington, Madison, and Franklin. Sargent, born in Vermont in 1823, lived in Massachusetts and Illinois before arriving in Red Wing in 1856. His first stay at Wastedo was brief. Within two years he moved back to Red Wing and thence to a farm in Burnside township. He did return to Wastedo for a time in the 1860s.

Although Terrell's dreams of a metropolis never materialized and he moved to Lake City in a few years, the town he started did not vanish. Even Mitchell wrote that Martin Thompson built a second store in 1858 that thrived even after Sargent's was out of business. The post office also remained. Ellery Stone succeeded Sargent as postmaster on August 17, 1858, but Sargent returned on January 26, 1864. He did not finally leave the post until December 10, 1866, when Israel Stone replaced him. Edward G. Bailey became postmaster on November 25, 1867, but held the job only until June 29 of the following year. Then Martin Thompson took the job. Born in Norway in 1837, Thompson ar-

One of the stores in Wastedo. *GCHS*

rived in the United States just in time to participate in the Civil War. He ran a store at Wastedo until 1889, six years before his death. His enlistment papers and the 1869 county history give his name as Thompson, but his full name was Martin T. Opsal, and through most of his stay at Wastedo he was known by that name. In retirement he settled in Cannon Falls, where he had lived earlier. In 1869 he had the only store in Leon township; reportedly it sold between $10,000 and $15,000 worth of goods annually.

An 1873 gazetteer listed Thompson's store as the only business place at Wastedo, but by 1878 two stores and a blacksmith shop were listed. By that time there had been two changes in the post office. On March 24, 1874, Carl O. Johnson replaced Thompson. Gustaf A. Ryden (or Rydin) succeeded Johnson on July 26, 1876. Ryden, formerly in business at Hader, apparently had erected a store building that year, believed to be the one housing the Wastedo store until 1965. Unlike the two earlier stores, this was in section 22, east of the plat laid out by Terrell. The other store operating in 1878 was that of Opsal. The blacksmith, first in the village, was Elias Erickson, also known as Elias Rosvold. The postmastership went on December 13, 1880, to Andrew A. Beaurline, but he held the office only about a month. Opsal followed on January 17, 1881. The Ryden store passed to the firm of Sandberg & Rosing in 1880 and subsequently, it appears, to Beaurline, who on August 21, 1883, again became postmaster. The postmastership (and probably the store) went in 1886 to Lewis J. Johnson, who for some years ran the store in partnership with Edward Anderson.

During Johnson's long postmastership, Wastedo filled a role of importance in the local economy. Besides the store (Johnson & Anderson), there was a blacksmith shop run by Charles Berggren, previously in business at White Rock, from at least 1882 until the end of the century. (According to the 1880 census, Frederick Carlson ran a blacksmith shop there earlier.) In the later 1890s the village also had two sorghum mills, as well as a music teacher and two ministers receiving mail at the Wastedo post office. A. Haggstrom operated a feed mill there by 1887. A town hall was built in 1894. A correspondent for the

The same store in 1964. *RWM*

Kenyon Leader in 1897 painted this picture of the busy settlement: "Our little town shows quite a lively attitude with the mill grinding every day and the merry ring of the anvil. Friday the hitching posts were lined with teams whose owners came here to do business." Apparently Wastedo had only one store at that time, however, for in 1892 Johnson had bought "what is known as the Opsal store property."

Despite economic changes detrimental to its interests, Wastedo nearly held its own in the early years of the 20th century. In the year the post office closed, 1903, a group of local farmers organized the Wastedo Creamery Company. Building commenced during the winter, and by the end of June the creamery building was ready for business. F. S. Stone of Northfield and his brother, S. E. Stone, operated it first, with I. O. Dybevick of Lake Crystal its buttermaker. Longtime storekeeper Lewis J. Johnson had organized a telephone company in 1897 that upon his death in 1911 was worth $10,000.

Gradually, however, Wastedo lost ground. The post office went first. Johnson, who had become postmaster on December 29, 1886, retained the office until it closed, on October 31, 1903. In 1907 the feed mill closed for several months, and the next year it went up for sale. In the years following, the blacksmith shop and the creamery closed. Oscar Nygaard used the creamery building as a garage and repair shop for some 40 years before it closed too. The telephone company outlasted most of the other businesses, but it finally merged with a larger exchange. The store, run for a quarter century by Andrew Hanson and later by Harris and Lucelle Nelson and by Mrs. Dan (Viola) Kvamme, closed in 1951. After three-and-a-half years, however, the store reopened in December 1954 under Edward Kleiber, who ran it for the next decade. The four-lane highway that disrupted the remnants of Hader affected Wastedo even more severely, for it required the removal of the store—closed and torn down in the spring of 1965. Later that year the old creamery building was razed, and a rural school, converted to a dwelling in the 1950s, was moved to a new site. The town hall, replaced by a new structure some distance from the original site of Wastedo, went to a neighboring farm.

Although business activity in Terrell's paper city has ended and only two houses remain to mark the site, the name promises to survive for awhile. When Goodhue County's rural school system reorganized in the 1950s, the residents of the Wastedo area set up a consolidated district and erected a new school a mile east of the cluster of houses at the site of old Wastedo. When this school gave way to further consolidation, the building became Goodhue County Education District 6051–61, a school for emotionally disturbed children bused in from other districts in the county.

State Senator A. J. Rockne of Zumbrota once said the name *Wastedo* derived from an Indian word meaning *good*. There may be something to this explanation, for the Riggs *Grammar and Dictionary of the Dakota Language*

(1852) gives *wa-ste-da* as a verb meaning "to esteem good, to love." Terrell may have picked up the word, modified it to suit his purposes, and applied it to the town he imagined.

White Rock

In the same year that the Vasa Farmers' Union formed (1868), a group of farmers in the southern part of Vasa township organized the "Farmers' Commercial Union" and built a store similar to that at Vasa village. This store formed the nucleus of a hamlet along the Vasa-Belle Creek township line and on both sides of the stream called Belle Creek. Because of a rock formation nearby, the locality became known as "White Rock," and the post office opening there in 1871 took that name. Mons F. Monson, who had managed the farmers' store from its inception, became postmaster of the new office on December 8.

Like Vasa, White Rock was never platted into blocks and streets. It developed more or less haphazardly, as merchants, artisans, and professional men came to settle there. It did not grow rapidly at first. An 1873 gazetteer listed only one businessman, a druggist calling himself Dr. C. E. Bolander, in addition to the store managed by Monson. Five years later, however, the White Rock post office served two blacksmiths, a stonemason, a carpenter, a boot- and shoemaker, a saddle- and harnessmaker, a tailor, and a currier (tanner). Monson

The G. O. Miller store, built in White Rock in 1883. *GCHS*

was proprietor of a general store, which suggests that the farmers' group had dissolved and that its store had come into his possession. By 1880 John Westerson (or Westerton), appointed postmaster on March 5, 1879, was running the store. The census of that year reported the same businesses as the 1878 gazetteer, plus a store run by Julius Wester and a third blacksmith shop. All but two of the nine men listed were born in Sweden.

White Rock had only three postmasters during its 32 years. After serving in that capacity for nearly five years, Westerson gave way to Gustaf O. Miller on February 19, 1886. Miller, who had earlier served as postmaster at Finney, came to White Rock in 1883 and entered the general merchandise business. From then until his death in 1933 he was closely identified with the village. He was its principal merchant until 1907, the founder of the G. O. Miller Telephone Company, and moving spirit behind the White Rock Creamery Association and White Rock State Bank. Chiefly due to his efforts, White Rock did not simply fade away like so many others.

An 1886–87 gazetteer listed four businesses in White Rock: Miller's store, G. Carlson's saloon, Gilbert S. Strom's blacksmith shop, and P. Olson's shoe- and harnessmaking establishment. With some changes in personnel, the list remained the same until 1890–91, when the saloon disappeared. There were no changes in the biennial gazetteers until the 1898–99 volume added Benson & Johnson's feed mill. But a creamery had started in 1887, and there may have been other unlisted businesses.

In 1892 William H. Westerson, a student at Pine Island High School, wrote an essay on "My Native Town," offering the following picture:

> In Section 32 is located the small village of White Rock, where the famous White Rock creamery is located, whose product is known from New York to Tacoma. Here is the general store of G. O. Miller, who keeps ten teams busy collecting cream and delivering goods.

Two years later Miller built a store 30 by 60 feet, with a grocery department in front and a creamery in the basement. In 1895 another building went up to the west to house the post office and part of the stock. At that time the creamery was turning out 4,500 pounds of butter a week. From there it went to Cannon Falls, where Miller had a warehouse on the Milwaukee railroad. Besides the blacksmith and the harness and shoe-repair shops (which also provided meals to travelers), White Rock had a Swedish Baptist chapel, erected in the 1880s.

In 1900 the White Rock chapter of the Modern Woodmen of America built a hall for public meetings as well as lodge affairs. A sorghum mill was in operation a couple of years later, and in 1907 the G. O. Miller Company incorporated with a capital stock of $50,000. Despite the prosperity of the village, the post office had closed October 31, 1903, to be replaced by rural carrier from Cannon Falls. The loss of its post office did not affect White Rock so severely as other communities in the same circumstance. The creamery still operated in 1908 and apparently for some years afterward. The telephone company, dating from 1907, remained in operation many years.

In the middle of the next decade White Rock experienced a minor burst of business activity. Like Frontenac, Bellechester, Skyberg, Stanton, and Welch, it acquired a bank in that era. On June 21, 1915, the White Rock State Bank incorporated, with Per A. Peterson as president, E. P. Erickson vice president, Ed Erickson cashier, and C. E. Swanson assistant cashier. By June 30, 1920, the bank had resources of $113,224.27. Unlike most of other small-town banks, the White Rock bank did not fail then or during the Great Depression. Still thriving at the end of the 20th century, it had expanded to include branches at Cannon Falls and Bellechester.

The bank was not the only evidence of life in White Rock. The Strom blacksmith shop, which had a harness shop upstairs, was later run by John Lindberg. Businesses dependent on horses closed down with the advent of the tractor and the automobile, replaced by ones adapted to the new order. A garage/blacksmith shop built by Nels Martenson and his son Harry in 1916 or 1917 went to Edwin Anderson in 1924. He and his son Edsel ran it as a garage, selling Star, Durand, and Maxwell automobiles. In 1948, they built a new garage on the west end of the village. After Edsel left the business in 1973, it had other owners. After a fire in the early 1990s, it closed.

Why the revival of White Rock business activity more than a decade after its post office closed? The proposal to build an interurban rail line from St. Paul to Rochester via Hastings, Miesville, Cannon Falls, White Rock, and Zumbrota probably was the impetus. Completed as far as Hastings by the St. Paul Southern Electric Railway and graded somewhat farther in 1914–16, the project faltered when the company went into receivership in 1918. A decade later it became totally insolvent and terminated its service to Hastings.

White Rock did not emerge unscathed from more recent economic change. The G. O. Miller general store closed during World War II, leaving only one store in the village. The Martenson family ran it for many years in a former hotel erected in 1916 by Ferdie and Esther Martenson. Le Roy McCusker operated it later. Its last owner was Leo McKenna. When McKenna drowned in a flood that struck the area in 1978, the store closed, and the Goodhue fire department burned it in 1981. The Baptist church has long since disappeared, and the village now has neither church nor school. The White Rock hall, scene of meetings and other activities for many years, has come into private possession and now is used for storage. Ten occupied houses and the flourishing White Rock State Bank are all that remain of the village of White Rock.

White Willow

Like several other post offices in Goodhue County, White Willow originated along a stage line, then moved to meet the railroad coming through. In this case, the move did not occur until a thriving community with a name of its own had grown up at the railroad station.

On January 5, 1876, Peter Peterson, a blacksmith living in the northeast quarter of section 9, Zumbrota township, applied to the Post Office Department for a new post office—White Willow. He claimed it would serve about 400 patrons. The department responded quickly, for on January 13 he became postmaster at the new office, about a rod from the Red Wing-Zumbrota road, roughly followed by T.H. 58 today. Although a rural school stood nearby and early gazetteers list a carpenter, mason, and book agent receiving mail at White Willow, no village then developed. Peterson, a Danish immigrant then in his early twenties, had married a woman several years his senior who previously was married to a man named Wilks. Their household in 1880 included her 17-year-old daughter by the earlier marriage and two younger children born of her marriage to Peterson. On January 8, 1885, the postmastership passed to Olaf O. Nordvold, who kept the office in his farm home not far from the earlier site.

The construction in 1889 of the Duluth, Red Wing & Southern Railroad from Red Wing to Zumbrota changed the destiny of the White Willow post office. A station named Rice (honoring the Rev. W. C. Rice, a Zumbrota minister who owned land in the vicinity and who was an official of the railroad company) opened about two miles west of the post office. Soon a busy trading center grew up around the point where the railway crossed the wagon road along the line between sections 5 and 6. A grain elevator, a hotel, and a general store began operation in 1890, then a second elevator, a tavern, a cream separator, a stockyard, and a feed mill.

The anomaly of a rural post office providing mail to a developing railroad town two miles away (the mail came in on the train) apparently took a while to sink in. The government advertised in the summer of 1889 for bids to carry the mail from Rice's station to the White Willow post office three times a week. By the end of 1890, however, Thomas Moran, proprietor of the new store, applied to have the post office removed and himself made postmaster. On February 25, 1891, his appointment became effective, and the post office took up residence at Rice station. For a time there was confusion about the community's two names, especially since there was a Rice post office elsewhere in Minnesota. The problem ended when the railroad changed the name of its station to White Willow.

Moran remained in charge of the store for less than two-and-a-half years. With his departure from the business, the post office changed hands. On September 12, 1893, Frederick H. Hinz, who had been running the store for several months, replaced him. By the next November Hinz reportedly was selling out. Frank Laverne leased the store and ran it for less than a year. He turned it over to Hans O. Holstad, formerly of Hader, who ran it for the next four years. Changes in the post office did not always reflect these transfers of ownership. Hinz stayed on as postmaster only until March 27, 1894, when Ed Woodbury took the job. Woodbury, employed as grain buyer by one of the elevators, declined the office, and on September 26 that year, Holstad took over.

Coincidental with Holstad's appointment, the spelling of the post office's name officially changed to *Whitewillow*, in accordance with the department's policy of combining double names when possible. White Rock, Hay Creek, Spring Creek, Fair Point, and (temporarily) even Red Wing also suffered the practice, which the department never explained.

One further change of postmaster occurred at Whitewillow. Late in 1898, Holstad sold his store to Herman Zemke, whose son, Charles J. Zemke, took over management of the store and became postmaster on January 14, 1899. The original store had burned the previous April, but apparently Holstad replaced it that summer. The younger Zemke, also manager of the Minnesota Malting Company's elevator and half-owner of a coal business, remained postmaster until the office closed, on February 28, 1905. Whitewillow was the last Goodhue County post office to succumb to RFD. Not until 1934 was another office existing in 1905 discontinued, though in the intervening three decades one (Bellechester) had come and gone.

White Willow still flourished at the time the post office closed. The previous fall, in response to a citizens' petition, the State Railroad and Warehouse

The buttermaker's home at White Willow.
Later it was a "blind pig"—providing bootleg liquor. *GCHS*

The cheese factory of the White Willow Dairy Association. *GCHS*

Commission found the railroad station doing an annual business in excess of $12,000. The commission ordered a "standard depot building" to replace the freight shed that heretofore served the community. In 1908, a rumor that White Willow was to be reduced to a flag station—where trains stopped only when someone flagged them down—proved false. In the years following, the prosperity of the village perceptibly declined, one business place disappearing after another. White Willow was too close to Goodhue, which by 1900 had a population of 241—a figure that nearly doubled in the next decade. Business gravitated towards the larger community, and White Willow lost ground.

In March 1912 an auctioneer advertised the stock of the Zemke store, said to be going out of business. Four years later the county sheriff sold the building at a foreclosure sale. White Willow seemed about to die. The Minnesota Malting Company's grain elevator, closed in 1914, went up for sale two years later. An advertisement spoke of its value as lumber—enough to build a nearly complete set of farm buildings. Herman Leach bought the building early in 1917 and tore it down. Two years earlier there had been a report that the depot might be closed. "Get out your handkerchief," advised the *Goodhue Enterprise*, "not to shed a tear, but [to] flag the train in case you want to climb on and go some place."

But White Willow was not finished. Not only was the report about the depot premature (Miss Agnes Schafer was mentioned as station agent in May 1917), but on March 10, 1916, a group of local farmers organized the White

Willow Dairy Association. Soon thereafter it built a cheese factory, opened for business in June. During 1917 it bought 1,062,428 pounds of milk. Perhaps encouraged by this revival of business, the store reopened. In November 1916 Richard Winter of New York had bought the building from Charles Zemke. Soon it too would open for business.

This turned out to be the dying gasp of White Willow business activity. Winter closed the store again in 1920. Meanwhile, the second elevator also closed; it was torn down about 1922. Local newspapers did not mention it, but according to former residents, the store operated briefly one summer—probably in 1925—under two young men named Vieths and Spring (or Springer). A visitor reported it vacant in 1926. The cheese factory remained in operation long after all the other businesses, but on June 4, 1938, the White Willow Dairy Association sold out to the Farmers' Cooperative Butter and Cheese Association of Zumbrota. The factory stood idle until the spring of 1939, when most of it was torn down. Portions of its walls remained a few years longer.

The depot lasted for many years after the agency closed in 1919; it was not removed until the later 1930s. A sign along the tracks replaced the depot, but before long that too disappeared. In 1965 the railroad line was abandoned, and soon thereafter the rails and ties were removed. One by one, most of the houses in White Willow disappeared. When the old store building, long used as a residence, was dismantled and moved in 1948, the *Zumbrota News* announced: "White Willow Is No More."

4

Some Concluding Observations

Anyone reading the sketches of discontinued post offices in Goodhue County probably recognizes that they are also sketches of the small rural villages of the county, containing detail of only casual relevance to their postal histories. The reason is obvious. The services performed by the rural post offices were analogous to those performed by the villages themselves. And the reasons for their demise—at least in the 20th century—were much the same as the reasons for the decline of the villages.

In an era of relatively heavy rural population and horse-drawn communication, post offices and local trading centers necessarily were located at frequent intervals through the countryside. When the rural population declined and better means of communication (of which RFD was one) became available, the need for these conveniences diminished. The mail came to the farmer's door, and the farmer drove to the nearest sizable town, where competition among merchants freed him or her from the monopoly prices and lesser variety of country stores. Cheese factories and creameries sprang up even in these latter days because nearby outlets for milk remained an advantage into the automobile age. But their day of prosperity—mostly in the second and third decades of the 20th century—was brief. During the 1930s and later, the consolidation and expansion of larger firms killed off the rural dairy plants.

Some farmers regretted the closing of rural post offices, but most of the opposition came from postmasters. They represented but a small minority whose motives could scarcely be regarded as disinterested. Most farmers were happy to receive carrier-delivered mail. They worried little about a loss of identity for their rural communities. Likewise, they showed only sporadic loyalty to the local storekeepers—or even to their own dairy cooperatives—when they could benefit by taking their trade elsewhere. Hence in the 20th century there was a steady erosion of community identity in the villages. After a farmer's address became Cannon Falls or Kenyon or Zumbrota, he or she soon identified with that town rather than with Wastedo or Aspelund or Roscoe Center.

School reorganization in the 1950s administered the final stroke in this progressive loss of rural community identity. Talk of an "expanded concept of community," together with the representation of farmers on consolidated school boards, brought the farm population into closer association with the towns. Most rural hamlets had had district schools, where local people met on school and nonschool business, reaffirming their sense of community. Now these schools were torn down or remodeled into dwellings, the school meetings held in the towns. Township halls located in a few of the hamlets came to serve almost exclusively as voting places.

In short, the concept of community has expanded. The term no longer applies, in Goodhue County at least, to 50 or 60 families living within a few miles' radius of a crossroads hamlet serving as a trading center and social gathering place. It may refer instead to an aggregation of hundreds, perhaps thousands, of families, some grouped in a town, the rest scattered over three or four townships. The individual may know personally only a fraction of the other members of this community, especially if he or she lives on a farm. The closest ties may not be with the nearest neighbors but with relatives or business associates in town or on farms some distance away.

Under such conditions, the old sense of community identity cannot survive, and the nodes of settlement, formerly the core of community, largely lose their reasons for being. When a local storekeeper happens to be a stranger to the locality, the farmers' feeling of loyalty diminishes, and they give up all pretense of trading "at home." And when its last business place closes down, a village is as good as dead, unless it has an active church to preserve the sense of community among its members. But the rural church has suffered a decline parallel to that of the villages. A study of the abandoned rural churches of Goodhue County would show similar patterns. In some respects it would reveal more, for the rural church, unlike the rural post office, usually is not subject to arbitrary decisions by a remote centralized authority. Thus it can be more responsive to local wishes.

The rural post office flourished under a specific set of conditions, some of which still prevail in some parts of the United States. It died in Goodhue County when those conditions ceased to prevail. The small rural trading center has followed a parallel course. Because a stroke of the pen cannot extinguish a village as easily as a post office, some "general stores" continued for half a century after the loss of the post offices. The principal stock of some of these consisted of beer, soft drinks, cigarettes, and candy, while others derived most of their income from sales of gasoline and other automotive products to highway motorists passing through. Those still in business maintained a precarious existence, and nearly all have since closed their doors. We may say, "Long may they live!" But we cannot ignore the probability that they will not. These survivors are anachronisms—their function now largely usurped by other methods of merchandising.

Other types of businesses suffered even greater mortality. Gristmills at such places as Cascade, Belvidere Mills, Forest Mills, and Hay Creek were among the first to expire. Blacksmith shops have long since disappeared from the crossroads hamlets. Gasoline stations, garages, and repair shops survived in a few places, such as Bellechester, Bombay, Sogn, and White Rock. Except for the Bellechester garage, however, all were gone by year 2000. Grain elevators, once common in the railroad villages, have vanished except at Bellechester and Bombay. Of the creameries and cheese factories once dotting the countryside, none carry on their original business. Those at Aspelund, Bellechester, Belvidere Mills, Bombay, Eggleston, Fair Point, Forest Mills, Hader, Lena, Nansen, Roscoe, Roscoe Center, Skyberg, Sogn, Stanton, Vasa, Wangs, Wastedo, White Rock, and White Willow have closed. The one at Belle Creek is now a feed store.

Sometimes a place name survives after the entity is gone. Road maps may include the names of communities that travelers can barely find on the ground. Other times, mapmakers drop the names of places still alive. The most recent (2000) state highway map lists Bellechester, Belvidere Mills, Bombay, Hader, Hay Creek, Roscoe, Sogn, Vasa, Wacouta, Wangs, and White Rock. As late as 1964, Aspelund, Nansen, and Wastedo were shown. An oil company map published by Rand McNally in the 1960s listed all these plus Claybank, Eggleston, Fairpoint, Harlis, and Skyberg. A similar map published by the H. M. Gousha Company omitted several of these but included Roscoe Center and Forest Mills. The most recent (1993) revision of the county map published by the Minnesota Department of Transportation includes all of these but Fairpoint, Eggleston, Nansen, and Roscoe Center, and it adds Belle Creek, Lena, and Ryan.

In a sense, a community retains its identity so long as it appears on a map. It exists in a more complete sense when there are identifying signs along a road at or near the place itself. A policy adopted about 1960 by the Minnesota Highway Department (its name at the time) contributed to the loss of identity in villages along state highways. Within a few months, identifying signs disappeared from highways passing through Bombay, Hay Creek, Skyberg, Wangs, and Wastedo. Later the signs at Bombay and Hay Creek were restored, the latter spelled *Haycreek*. Signs still identify Hader and Vasa. Others point to Belle Creek, Aspelund, Belvidere Mills, Roscoe, and White Rock, all off the highways, but these may not stand much longer. Unlike some others, Goodhue County has not bothered in recent years to erect signs identifying these villages along local roads, though in a few cases private parties have done so. The county did erect mileage signs at crossroads near Vasa, White Rock, Sogn, and perhaps other communities off main highways, but some of these are now gone.

In any case, a road sign is no substitute for the once-present vitality of these small communities. For many of them, the loss of identity stems from the closing of the post office. In some instances, the modest compensation derived from the postal business represented the difference between profit and loss for the storekeeper, who gave up the store when this source of revenue was lost. Doomed by changes in the economy, in transportation, and in communication, some of these villages lost their souls with their post offices. Some lingered on in increasing debility for 20, 30, perhaps 40 years. Some still give the appearance of mild prosperity, mainly because empty buildings are razed so as not to testify to pervading decay.

Something more than simple nostalgia for an era never known and dimly imagined moves those who regret the decline of the crossroads villages and the communities centered there. They see a loss in human values that the "expanded concept of community" does not replace. With all its parochialism and provincialism, the small rural community provided its members with a sense of personal significance that larger aggregations do not offer. At the same time it gave them a group identity and the possibility of knowing every member well. Belongingness and togetherness were neither elusive goals sought by devious means nor slick advertising slogans. Neither was the individual in ferment about threats to his or her individuality.

Perhaps even the provincialism of these communities has been exaggerated. One cannot know the content of those debates in the Roscoe school, but the topics selected do not suggest a population ignorant of the issues of the day. In some Norwegian communities in Goodhue County, the people had access to traveling libraries containing books in both Norwegian and English. The number of those going on to distinguish themselves suggests that their surrounding societies nurtured their native abilities. In fact, unless we suppose that these individuals were "giants in the earth," their communities must have been unusually favorable to their development.

The rural post offices are gone, and the small villages are dead or dying—both having "outlived their usefulness." Both served earlier generations well. Who is prepared to state categorically that the institutions and way of life that replaced them are doing or will do as much?

References

1. Its chief promoter, Henry Ahneman, settled in 1856 on the northeast quarter of section 23, Pine Island township. Mossville, therefore, probably was on or near the St. Paul and Dubuque road, about three miles southeast of Poplar Grove. Several early settlers in that vicinity went by the name Maas; Ahneman probably intended the name *Maasville*.
2. For more information on the CGW's Bellechester branch, see my study, "The Railroads of Goodhue County" (1984), pp. 128–31, typewritten manuscript, Goodhue County Historical Society, Red Wing.
3. A post office named Troy opened in southwestern Winona County on June 15, 1858. It served until April 29, 1905.
4. Many Norwegian immigrants used the Scandinavian patronymic (ending in *son* or *sen*) and another name, commonly a place name in Norway. Thus the 1877 county map shows in Wanamingo township alone such names as Peter Olson Barsness, Torsten Anderson Aaby, Erick Nelson Eidvaag, Lars Sorenson Hjermstad, Erick Erickson Sevareid, and Henry Nelson Talla. Some went by one name during one period and by another name later. Such practices made for complications in identifying certain residents of Holden, Wangs, Wastedo, and other places settled by Scandinavians.
5. The Elmira plat also shows a Water Street. This commonly encountered street name usually borders a lake or river. Since the only running water on this prairie site is what flows immediately after a heavy rain, one might question the appropriateness of the name.
6. The Huberty cheese factory, also in Pine Island township, started the same year. The subject of the cheese industry in Goodhue and neighboring counties awaits scholarly investigation.
7. On the Sewall map, Stanton shows as Fremont. To the author's knowledge, this is the only source identifying it as such.
8. The April 1993 issue of *Goodhue County Historical News* contains a detailed and lively description by Bruce Akerson of the Akerson store as it was in the 1930s. Akerson is the son of its longtime keeper.
9. Terrell's first claim, filed July 19, 1856, was the half section immediately east of this tract, the western half of section 22. But the plat clearly shows that the eastern half of section 21 was the first laid out.

Sources

James West says in his introduction to *Plainville U.S.A.* (New York: 1945) that even for such a town as "Plainville" (Wheatland, Missouri—population 269 in 1940), "there exists so vast a body of relevant printed or other documentary material that no one could read it all in a lifetime." If this is true of a single small Missouri town, it is certainly true of the ghost towns and discontinued post offices of Goodhue County. I do not profess to have read everything that might contain information relevant to my purposes, but I have looked at nearly all the obvious and at some not-so-obvious sources. The following list shows not only where I found information but also where the reader might find more.

Government Documents (Federal, State, County, and Township)
United States Post Office Department Registers of Appointments and Site Location Surveys constitute the basic source for postal data. They are now found in Record Group 28, Social and Economic Records, National Archives and Records Service. The Registers of Appointments, large buckram-bound volumes, contain the dates of establishment and discontinuance of post offices and the dates of appointment for postmasters. Except for Central Point, they seem to be complete for Goodhue County. Since they extend only to about 1931, information on subsequent changes is from correspondence with the Postmasters and Rural Appointments Division, Bureau of Operations, Post Office Department. The Site Location Surveys are fragmentary and include only a few post offices in Goodhue County. Where they exist, however, they give the location of an office plus some information on how it came to be established and how many patrons it was expected to serve.

The federal population schedules, Bureau of the Census, for 1860, 1870, and 1880 provide information on individuals not prominent enough to have been the subject of biographical sketches, except in hard-to-find newspaper obituaries. The Industrial Census for 1870 contains valuable data on mills, blacksmith shops, and other small industries. The schedules for these census years (as well as for 1850, 1840, and, partly, 1830), Record Group 29, are available on microfilm from the National Archives. For 1860, the schedules for all Minnesota counties from Anoka through Le Sueur are on Roll 126, Microcopy T-7. Most of the Minnesota schedules for 1870 burned in 1921, and the National Archives has microfilmed the state census schedules for that year. Those for Goodhue County (and several other counties) are on Rolls 4 and 5, Microcopy T-132. For 1880, the schedules for Goodhue County are on Rolls 620 and 621, Microcopy T-9, which includes Freeborn, Grant, and part of Hennepin counties as well.

The only state publications, apart from the 1870 census schedules, used for this study are the *Minnesota Executive Documents*, which contains various reports from state agencies. The reports of the Railroad and Warehouse Commission provide information on the organization of railroad companies, the construction of railroads, and, in the early years, statistics on revenue. The secretary of state's report contains the dates of filing for articles of incorporation. The state banking commissioner's reports contain much the same type of information on banks.

The most valuable county records are those in the Office of the County Recorder. The original plats of nearly all the county's villages and cities are found there. During my original research, in the 1960s, most were in a series of Books of Plats. Since then they have been transferred to a "hanging file." Articles of incorporation are found in the Miscellaneous Records, which occupy a large proportion of the office wall space. Another valuable source is a volume containing copies of the original land office entries. Through reference to these entries one may determine the exact tract or tracts on which some of the early postmasters filed claims. Since one may reasonably assume that they resided on their claims, the original locations of several early post offices can be fixed with fair certainty. Much of the northeastern part of the county was included in the Sioux Half-Breed Reserve, however, and there the names of the claimants are usually those of the "mixed-bloods" who nominally located scrip on some tracts but did not live there. The first white settlers purchased this scrip from those individuals, and their names do not appear in the records.

I made some use of the Goodhue County Board of Commissioners' "Proceedings" and tax lists, both housed in the County Auditor/Treasurer's Office; certain vital statistics records in the Office of the Court Administrator, District 1; and the records of the superintendent of schools. For a detailed description of these and other records, see Minnesota Historical Records Survey, Works Projects Administration, *Inventory of the County Archives of Minnesota: No. 25 Goodhue County* (St. Paul: 1941).

The Goodhue County Historical Society has township records and account books, most of them fragmentary, from 19 of the 23 townships. Only those from Belvidere, Roscoe, and Warsaw were used in this investigation. The records of at least a dozen townships extend back to 1860 or earlier. Since the early post-masters and town proprietors were in many cases also township officials, sketchy information is available in these records.

For an earlier study of Forest Mills, on which the present account is based, I used some of the records of School District 130, now in private hands.

Newspapers

In terms of time spent, by far the greatest part of my research took place in newspaper files. For most of the county weeklies, I have examined all extant issues before 1900. For some I followed the files a few years into the 20th century. For the *Kenyon Leader* and *Zumbrota News* I went through the entire backfiles. I have used a few newspapers in neighboring counties for information on towns like Cascade, Rest Island, and Skyberg, which were near the edge of Goodhue County. I have sampled the Red Wing dailies for the 1890s and the 20th century but have considered the task of plowing through all of them too time-consuming for the probable reward. Since 1940, however, I have kept a clipping file of items on the ghost towns of Goodhue County, including land-mark photos appearing in the *Red Wing Daily Republican Eagle* since the 1950s. A complete list of newspapers consulted follows.

> *Cannon Falls Beacon*
> *Goodhue Enterprise*
> *Goodhue County Tribune* (Goodhue)
> *Goodhue County Republican* (originally and later *Red Wing Republican*)
> *The Kenyon Leader*
> *Lake City Graphic-Sentinel*
> *Mazeppa Journal*
> *Minnesota Signal* (Kenyon)
> *Northfield Independent*
> *Pine Island Journal*
> *Pine Island Record*
> *REA Reflector* (Zumbrota)
> *Red Wing Argus*
> *Red Wing Daily Republican*
> *Red Wing Daily Republican Eagle*
> *Red Wing Sentinel*

Rice County Journal (Northfield)
West Concord Enterprise
The Zumbrota News

The dates of establishment of these newspapers, together with the dates of discontinuance for those that no longer exist, may be found in Winifred Gregory, *American Newspapers 1821–1936: A Union List of Files Available in the United States and Canada* (New York: H. W. Wilson, 1937).

Books and Articles

No one undertaking a local history project can avoid the use of county histories, despite their inadequacies. Which of Goodhue County's histories is most valuable depends on what one is looking for. None has been particularly thorough on the county's postal history, and the treatment of ghost towns varies greatly from one town to another in respect to completeness and accuracy. Most of the sketches of ghost towns can be traced back to the earliest history of the county, with the initial errors repeated and compounded in each succeeding book.

The county's first history was W. H. Mitchell's *Geographical and Statistical Sketch of the Past and Present of Goodhue County, together with a general view of the State of Minnesota* (Minneapolis: O. S. King, 1869). Because it was published only 16 years after the county was organized, it has the value of a primary source. Although much of the information it provides is now impossible to check for accuracy, the frequency of errors found in portions susceptible to validation render the rest suspect. Still, it is useful in the absence of other sources for some "facts." Much the same is true of the compilation *History of Goodhue County, Including a Sketch of the Territory and State of Minnesota* (Red Wing: Wood, Alley, 1878). Although the contributions vary with the industriousness of the contributor, some information here, especially in the biographies, is elsewhere unobtainable.

Joseph W. Hancock, the first permanent white settler in the county, published *Goodhue County, Past and Present* (Red Wing: Red Wing Printing, 1893) towards the end of his long career of public service. Informative on the Sioux (Dakota) people of the area, among whom Hancock was a missionary, and about Red Wing, where he lived most his life, this history tends to slight the outlying townships. In 1909 Goodhue County received the customary treatment of the period in a massive compilation edited by Franklyn Curtiss-Wedge. *History of Goodhue County, Minnesota* (Chicago: H. C. Cooper Jr.) is a 1,074-page volume including some new facts but lifting much of its material, especially on ghost towns, verbatim from predecessors. Its treatment of the county's postal history is the most nearly complete of those in county histories, but it still leaves much to be desired.

Christian A. Rasmussen's *A History of Goodhue County, Minnesota* (Red Wing: the author, 1935) should have been a much better book than it is. Rasmussen had the knowledge and command of style to do the definitive history of the county. Aside from Red Wing, however, which he had treated in a separate book, he failed to apply the most elementary principles of historiography to the evidence available. Instead, he largely repeated what the Curtiss-Wedge volume had repeated from Mitchell. Except for the sketches of Forest Mills and Sevastopol (the former the work of Sarah P. Hall of Zumbrota), he contributed nothing new on the ghost towns of Goodhue County.

The writing of Goodhue County's history came of age in the year 2000 with the publication of Frederick L. Johnson's *Goodhue County, Minnesota: A Narrative History* (Red Wing: Goodhue County Historical Society Press). Head and shoulders above its predecessors, Johnson's book shows what can be accomplished by a competent scholar free to follow his own bent, untrammeled by the hidebound traditions of local history. As William E. Lass says in his *Minnesota History* review of the book, "One can only hope that [Johnson's book] will become a model for other county historical societies that want to bring the history of their counties up to date." This is not to say, however, that Johnson's work entirely supersedes the earlier county histories. They continue to have value as sources of factual information—the raw data on which future generalizations can be based.

Although not exactly a county history, Harold Severson's *Goodhue County Heritage* (1963) contains some new information on industries in some of the smaller communities and, in its biographical sketches, on some of the people who contributed to their development. Likewise, the group production *Zumbrota: The First 100 Years* (Zumbrota: Zumbro Valley Historical Society, 1956) contains sketches of Forest Mills and of the four townships adjacent to Zumbrota. Both of these books are based in part on interviews and thus include some information that never reached the pages of the newspapers. Like the earlier county histories, however, they lack formal documentation. Of the same type is a pamphlet published at Cannon Falls in 1954 by the Centennial General Committee with the title *Historical Sketches of Cannon Falls 1854–1954*. It includes a picture of the original Oxford mill and an account of the mill lifted from the county histories.

Of several more recent local histories, the most notable are *Goodhue Diamond Jubilee, 1897–1972* (1972); Harold Severson, *We Give You Kenyon* (1976); *Memories of Wanamingo and Area* (1978); Margaret E. Hutcheson, *Goodhue: The Story of a Railroad Town* (1989); Carmen Johnson, *The Days of Dennison* (1992); and *Memories of Bellechester* (2000). Most of these include some mention of outlying communities.

The earlier-mentioned article on Forest Mills is one of two versions by the present author, the other published in *Minnesota History* 35 (March 1956):

11–21. Both are based on a 95-page typewritten history of Forest Mills, of which the Goodhue County Historical Society has a copy. An incomplete 12-page history of White Willow is appended. A valuable source of information on towns along the route of the Duluth, Red Wing & Southern Railroad Company is a series of two articles by James Burt, "The Red Wing Clay Line," in *North Western Lines* 18 (Fall 1991): 21–29; and 19 (Winter 1992): 48–61.

Certain other books that have been of use may be classified only as miscellaneous. These include Wayne E. Fuller, *R F D: The Changing Face of Rural America* (Bloomington: Indiana University, 1964), which mentions the opposition to rural free delivery by country postmasters, and Stephen R. Riggs, *Grammar and Dictionary of the Dakota Language* (Washington, D.C.: The Smithsonian Institution, 1852), referred to in the sketch of Wastedo. A book that came along more than a decade after the original version of the present work is Alan H. Patera and John S. Gallagher, *The Post Offices of Minnesota* (Burtonsville, Maryland: The Depot, 1978). At the time those authors were doing their research, the National Archives adopted a policy of barring the public from the stacks; they completed their work using microfilm copies of the documents.

Maps

Maps have been important to this study. Aside from unpublished town plats, the earliest is the *Sectional Map of the Surveyed Portion of Minnesota* issued by Joseph S. Sewall in 1857. Although it shows section lines, its scale is too small to reveal the locations of post offices with precision. Still, it tells approximately where they were. The Morris and Von Minden map (1861) is of too small a scale to be useful for the present purpose. Evidently it is based on the Sewall map, for it names the same towns and repeats the same errors (*Mineral* Springs for *Crystal* Springs, for example).

The next in order of time is *An Illustrated Historical Atlas of the State of Minnesota* (Chicago: Lakeside Building, 1874), edited by A. T. Andreas. Although it contains inaccuracies (*Ashland* for *Aspelund,* for example), it is the earliest work of its type and hence a tool indispensable to a study such as this. Walter W. Ristow tells the story of its production and distribution in "Alfred T. Andreas and His Minnesota Atlas," *Minnesota History* 40 (Fall 1966): 120–23.

In 1877 the firm of Warner and Foote prepared a detailed and surprisingly accurate map of the county, one of a series published at that time. The Goodhue County Historical Society's copy was later cut on township lines, mounted on stiff boards, and bound into the form of a plat book. A plat book of more orthodox design is C. M. Foote and J. W. Henion's *Plat Book of Goodhue County* (Minneapolis: C. M. Foote, 1894), which includes plats of several villages and a subscribers' directory.

Many plat books and atlases of the 20th century are undistinguished. De-signed primarily to show farm ownership, they are often careless about other details. The only ones meriting mention are *Atlas and Farmers' Directory of Goodhue County, Minnesota* (St. Paul: Webb Publishing, 1914) and *Atlas of Goodhue County, Minnesota* (Fergus Falls: Thomas O. Nelson, 1958).

Gazetters

Much use has been made of gazetteers. Most belong to one series. Although some information has been drawn from the *Minnesota State Gazetteer and Business Directory* (St. Paul: H. E. Newton, 1872) and its successors in the 1870s, most of the gazetteers consulted were of the series started by R. L. Polk of Detroit in 1879 and issued biennially well into the 20th century. Bearing the title of the earlier work, varied slightly from issue to issue, they contain the names of business and professional men, arranged by post office and spelled as they appear in handwritten sources.

Interviews

Many individuals have taken the trouble to provide me with information on communities familiar to them. Although newspapers usually make note of the opening of a new business place, they seldom record its closing and almost never mention when a long-abandoned building is torn down. For such facts and many others that never made their way into print, interviews and correspon-dence are indispensable.

Interviewing is a kind a research that can never be considered complete. There are always more people who could contribute information, by way of addition or correction to the story one is trying to tell. I can easily envision someone finding an error in this work and asking, "Why didn't he talk to me? I could have told him a lot more." The answers are that there are sources I never learned of, and if I followed up every possible lead, the work would never be published. One has to say "enough!" The work is never really done.

The recollections of the following have been most useful in filling in the gaps left by newspaper and other documentary research:

Carl J. Wangen (Aurland)
Donald T. Garrison (Belle Creek)
Arthur Diercks (Belvidere Mills)
Otto Drenckhahn (Belvidere Mills)
Mrs. Ray H. (Evelyn Wendler) Nelson (Eggleston)
Mrs. (Lenora) Erwin Bosshart (Fair Point)
Frank Charlton (Fair Point)
Orville Quimby (Fair Point)
Arthur Smith (Fair Point)

Mrs. Arthur Spreiter (Fair Point)
Herman Dahl (Forest Mills)
Mrs. Grace Dickey Scofield (Forest Mills)
Mrs. (Mabel) Philip J. Finnesgaard (Holden)
L. H. Underdahl (Nansen)
Virgil Henschel (Roscoe)
Mrs. (Berdella) Kenneth Syverson (Roscoe)
John V. McNamara (Ryan)
L. J. Erickson (Skyberg)
Adolph Stenhaug (Sogn)
Virgil Carlson (Vasa)
Earl Nelson (Vasa)
Glenn Olson (Vasa)
Edward Kleiber (Wastedo)
Pauline Nerison (White Rock)
Albert Prigge (White Willow)

Index

(Proper Names and Places)

Aaby, Torsten Anderson, 117
Aabye, Andrew L. 15
Abelson, Ole (Dr.), 80
Adams, Hugh, 98
AG Partners, 19
Ahlgren, Axel, 24
Ahneman, Henry, 117
Aiken, *see* Akin
Aiton, F. T., 7; John Felix (Rev.), 7
Akerson, Bruce, 117; Rudolph P., 96; store, *96*
Akin (Aiken), Daniel F., 32
Albert Lea, 4
Albrecht, Myrtle, 98; Raleigh, 98
Allandale, xi
Allen, Franklin M., 42; James, 30
American Legion, 18, 19
Amundson, John, 91
Anderson, A. V., 22; Anton, 33-35, *33, 35*; D. B., 51; E. C., 76; E. N., 22; Edsel, 107; Edward, 103; Edwin, 107; Martin M., 66; Pauline (Mrs. Anton), *33*; *see also* Johnson & Anderson
Andresen, August H., 84
Andrist, Godfrey, 49; Jacob, 76
Archer Daniels Midland (ADM), 28
Archibald family, 36
Archibald & Wilcox, mill, 36
Arco Dairies, 87
Arndt, Leonard, 16; Walter, 16
Arnold, Samuel, 55
Ashland, 11
Aslakson, P. S., 56
Aspelund, ix, x, 11-13, 114, 115, *iv, 10*; Emmanuel Lutheran Church, 11, 13, *12*; mercantile association, 11; Society, 11; store, *12*
Aurland, xi, 13, 14, 64, 68; Wangen Prairie Lutheran Church, 13
Austin, E. J., 33; Thomas J., 100
Ayr, xi, 14, 15, 44, 75

Babbitt, Samuel T., 55
Bailey, Carrie, 89; Edmund S., 31, 89; Edward G., 101; John V. H., 54
Bailey & Collins, mill, 31
Bakko, xi
Bang, Henry J., 24
Bank Holiday of 1933, 18

Banker's Honey, bee-keeping, 87
Barn Bluff, 7
Barker, Samuel A., 7
Barr, Ed, 67, 68
Barr, x, 67; Brick & Tile Co., 67
Barrett, Herman L., 38
Barsness, Guy, 86; Peter Olson, 117
Bartlett family, 95
Beaurline, Andrew A., 90, 103
Beckwith, Truman, 45
Befort, N. H., 19
Belle Chester, *see* Bellechester
Belle Creek (creek), 94, 105
Belle Creek, ix, x, 20-22, 42, 115; Cooperative Creamery Co., 22; Gardens, 22; Mercantile Cooperative Co., 22; St. Paul's Episcopal Church, 20, *21*; twp., 20, 22, 25, 30, 31, 79, 105
Bellechester, ix, x, 15-20, 25, 93, 107, 109, 115, 117; Community Center Association, 17; Coonie's Place, 19; Cooperative Creamery, 17, 19; Corner Grocery, 19; Counter's Bar, 17, 19; Garage, 17, 19; Haas's Bar, 19; Main Street, *16*; Nick's Place, 19; St. Mary's Church, 16
Bellechester Junction, xi
Belvidere, 23, 93; Cooperative, 24; twp., 15, 41, 45, 54, 93
Belvidere Mills, ix, 23-25, 36, 115; post office, *23*
Benrud, Marlin, 19; Oryen, 19
Benson, & Johnson, mill, 106; H. H., 89
Berg, Edmund, 22, 40
Berger, Nancy, 98; Norman, 98
Berget, J. O., 63
Berggren, Charles, 103
Bergo & Catlin, store, 14
Betcher Lumber Co., 17
Big Cannon River, 31
Billings, Harvey F., 88; Henry M., 88; *see also* Blackmer & Billings
Bjerva, Charles J. (Christian), 99
Bjorgo, John G., 14
Bjorgo & Catteye, store, 14
Black Oak, 25, 30, 79
Blackmer & Billings, harness makers, 46
Blagsvedt, William, 86

Blasdell, Edward, 46
Bolander, C. E. (Dr.), 105
Bols, — (Mr.), 47
Bombay, viii-x, 25-29, 86, 88, 89, 115; Dairy Co., 27; depot, *26*; Farmers Mercantile & Elevator Co., 27
Bonhus, Gunder, 8
Borlaug, Botolf J., 69, 70
Bosshart, Lenora (Mrs. Erwin), 124
Boyum, Bruce, 28; Steve, 28
Bradley, John H., 88
Brandvold, Brothers, store, 84; Able P., 84; R. P., 84, 85
Brekke, B. O., 100; Brothers, store, 100
Bremer, Elmer, 40
Briggs, Leonard, 88
Brokke, Augun H., 63
Brown, Carry (Carey) D., 14; James G., 8; Samuel L., 88; W. P., 52
Brusegaard, & Olson, store, 99; Thomas, 99
Brynhildsen, Hans L., 95
Buchholz, August, 75
Bugge, Jens, 88
Bullard, Elizabeth (Post), 97; George W., 97
Bundlie, Iver, 22
Burch, George, 91
Burgdorf, William, 59
Burkard, Albert, 17
Burkard, Albert A.(Sr.), 59, 60; Goodhue County House/Hotel, 60, *61*; family, 62; store, *61*
Burleigh (Burley), Ezekiel, 29
Burley, 29, 30, 50; school, 29, 30, *29*
Burns, see Byrnes
Burnside twp., 42
Burr Oak, 30
Burr Oak Springs, 20, 30, 31
Byrnes, John, 32; Thomas, 32

Callister, George, 48
Cannon City, 48
Cannon Falls, 7, 30, 31, 55, 57, 90, 106, 107, 114
Cannon Junction, xi
Cannon River, 8, 22, 31, 32
Cannon River Falls, 7, 30
Cannon Valley, 31, 32; Stock Farm, 31; Trail, 22

Carlson, & Hibbard, store, 76;
    Frederick, 103; G., 106; John
    W., 76; Virgil, 125
Carpenter, Samuel, 66
Cascade, 31-37, 89, 90, 115, *35*;
    cornet band, 34; Dramatic &
    Amateur Co., 34; fire, 34;
    Granville mills, 31, 32, 35, 89;
    Literary Society, 34; Manufac-
    turing Co., 32
Casper, Anthony M., 16; John, 16;
    Joseph H., 16
Catlin, & Brother, store, 14;
    Harvey (a.k.a. J. Harvey, Jo-
    seph H.), 14, 75, 76; Henry,
    14; Newland, 14
Central Point, 3, 38, 39; mill, 38;
    school, 38; twp., 38, 72
Chance, John, 7
Chandler, Betsy, 21; family, 20,
    21; Samuel P., 20
Charlson, Jonas, 26, 85; Marcus,
    26, 85; Rudolph, 86
Charlson Brothers & Otterness,
    store, 27, 86
Charlton, Frank, 124; *see also*
    Kelsey & Charlton
Cherry Grove twp., x, 14, 27, 44,
    88
Chester twp., Wabasha Co., 15
Christensen, Hans (a.k.a.
    Christianson; Hans
    Christianson Westermo), 44
Church, Elizabeth, 97
Churches, 114; Baptist, 94, 95,
    106, 107; Catholic, 79; Episco-
    pal, 20, *21*; Evangelical, 50;
    Lutheran, 11, 13, 16, 46, 63,
    72, 78, 93, 95, *12*, *71*; Method-
    ist, 37, 46, 75, 91, 92, 93, 95;
    Methodist Episcopal, 89
Clark, Prentiss M., 21, 42
Clay industry, 39, 40, 67
Clay Pits, xi, 39
Claybank, ix, x, 22, 39, 40, 115;
    Farmers' Grain Co., 40; store/
    depot, 40, *39*
Colburn Brick & Tile Co., 67
Cochran, Thomas T., 55
Coghlan, William, 38
Coleman, Myron F., 64
Collins, G., 55; Samuel, 31
Commander Elevator Co., 19, 28,
    91
Comstock, Israel T., 14, 15
Conrad, Joseph, 19
Corrigan, Joe, 82; Vera R. (Mrs.),
    82
Crawford, Joseph W., 38
Crescent Creamery Co., 13, 47,
    70, 76, 77, 90
Cross, Silas, 38
Crotten, Irv C., 86

Crouch, Cyrus, 45
Crystal Creamery Co., 13, 84
Crystal Springs, xi, 41; Farm, 41;
    twp., 41

Dack, Herman, 125; John, 90, 91;
    Mary, 90, 91
Dahl, P. E., 56
Dakota County, 32
Dakota (Sioux) Indians, 7; Con-
    flict of 1862, 75
Davidson, family, 28; John, 26,
    27; Michael J., 27, 28
Davidson, 26, 27
Day, D. D., 28
Dennison, 8, 33, 86, 90
Devlin, Bernard, 47
Dickey, Earl C. 48, 53; Jacob, 38;
    William Bruce, 51-53
Diercks, Arthur, 24, 124; John,
    24; Kurt, 40; William, 24
Dodson, Joseph N., 71
Dosdall Implement, 30
Dovre, 44
Doyle, Henry M., 30; Michael,
    30; Walter, 30
Drake, Arthur J., 32; Edwin S., 32
Drenckhahn, Otto, 124
Dressen, De Wayne, 62; James,
    62; Leo, Jr., 62; Saloon &
    General Mercantile, 62
Drew, Christopher R., 47
Drum, Caroline (Phares Bullard),
    97
Drurig (Durig), Frank, 54
Du Lac Co., 18
Dunkirk, 62
Dutch Oven, restaurant, 98
Dybevick, I. O., 104

Eagle Mills, 8, 41, 42
Eames, O., 97
Earl's Repair, 30
Easterly, Helen, 54; Hotel, 54;
    Peter, 45, 53, 54
Eastman, Herman, 45, 46
Eastman & Russell, store, 46
Eggleston, John E., 42; Joseph, 42
Eggleston, ix, 42-44, 115; Cream-
    ery & Produce Co., 43
Eidvaag, Erick Nelson, 117
Eidsvold, 44, 69
Eklund (Ecklund), Nels C., 95
Elder, John H., 98
Elliott, Joseph, 75
Ells, Edwin H., 81
Elmira, 44, 45, 50, 53, 54, 117
Engberg, Lewis, 93, 95; store, *94*
Engeberg, Ferdinand L., 95
Engelhart, —, *see* Mason, Olson
    & Engelhart
Epsom, 26

Erickson, E. P., 107; Ed, 107;
    Evald E., 83; L. J., 125
Erstad, Haugen & Co., store, 57
Ethel Howard, steamer, 73
Evenson, Even J., 99.

Faehn, Augustinius, 11
Fagen, xi
Fair Point (Fairpoint), ix-xi, 45-
    50, 80, 109, 115; Cooperative
    Cheese Association, 49;
    school, *49*
Fairbank, Henry E., 48
Faribault, 4, 8, 20, 25, 28, 53, 88
Farmers' Cooperative Butter &
    Cheese Association, 111
Farmers Elevator, 19
Farmers' Elevator Co., 82
Farmers State Bank, of
    Bellechester, 17; of Skyberg,
    81; of West Concord, 83
Farmers Union Grain Terminal
    Association, 28
Featherstone, 50; twp., 29, 50
Fennie, Nels, 82-84
Finnesgaard, Mabel (Mrs. Philip
    J.), 125
Finney, Jonathan, 50
Finney, x, 50, 51, 64, 106; twp.,
    50
Finseth Station, xi
Finstuen, Andrew, 77
Fish, Phineas S., 87
Fleischmann Malting Co., 19,
    28, 40
Flesche, Botolf O., 99; *see also*
    Melhuus & Flesche
Floan, Peter O., 70
Florence, 50, 51; twp., 38, 50
Flower Valley, xi
Forest Mills, viii, x, 35, 51-53,
    115
Forest Mills Co., flour mill, 52,
    51
Foster, Chancy, 33
Fox, Clifford, 57
Frederickson, Ray, 57
Fremont, 117
Fretheim, Peder, *85*
Friedemann, Caspar, 59
Frontenac, x, 3, 7, 50, 91, 107
Frost, Charles, 38
Fuller, Wayne E., 4

Gardner, Carter, 38
Garrison, Donald T., 22, 124; E.,
    46
Gatz, Gerhard, 54
Gay, George, 41
Gaylord, Nelson B., 23, 24
Geneva, 4
Gibson, C. B., 76; C. P. (Dr.),
    46; N. G. ("Hy"),

Gill, Harrison, 38
Gleason, John, 54
Glemme, *see* Stene & Glemme
Good, Jacob R., 74, 75
Goodhue, 8, 17, 41, 53, 54, 110;
  Cooperative Creamery, 59;
  twp., 8, 44, 45, 54
Goodhue Centre, 8, 45, 53, 54
Goodhue County, clay industry,
  39, 40, 67; Cooperative Elec-
  tric, 50, 78; county fair, 55;
  highways, 25, 28, 29; map, ii,
  iii; population, 3, 20; post
  offices, 4, 5, 7, 8; schools, 104
Goodhue State Bank, 18, 19
Goudy, William, 89, 90
Goxal, J. L., 56
Grannis, George H., 38; S. S., 38
Granville mills, *see* Cascade
Graasedelin, Nels O., 100
Great Depression, 18, 28, 67, 82,
  91, 107
Gronvold, Christian (Dr.), 70
Groven, Knut S., 70
Gullickson, Ole T., 66
Gustafson, John G., 93

Hack, John, 59
Hack & Meyer, mill, 59, 60
Hackett, Charles W. E., 38
Hader, ix, 55-59, 74, 76, 92, 101,
  104, 115; cheese factory, *58*;
  City Hotel, 56; Cooperative
  Cheese Association, 57, 58;
  store, *58*
Haggard, David M., 45, 46;
  Henry, 48; Thomas, 45, 46
Haggstrom, A., 103
Hagler, Fletcher, 74, 75
Haller, Edward, 57
Halvorson, B., 56
Hamand, H. O., 63
Hamery, Ludwig M., 100
Hammer creamery, *see* Zumbrota
Hancock, David, 4, 54
Hanson, Andrew, 57, 104; John
  O., 78; Thomas W., 55
Harlis/Harliss/Harlistown, xi, 115
Harrison, Elias S., 38; Hans, 56
Hart, S. A., 31
Hartman, Michael, 59
Hartville, xi
Hastings, 107
Haugen, Ole H., 66; Sivert O., 55-
  57; *see also* Erstad, Haugen &
  Co.
Hawkins, Edwin B., 38
Hay Creek, ix, x, 54, 59-62, 109,
  115; depot, *62*; mill, *60*; twp.,
  xi; valley, 40
Heber (Hieber), Nicholas, 16
Hegness, Edward, 76
Heigle, *see* Scherz & Heigle

Heltne, Martin P., 11
Henning, Peter A., 11-13
Henry, Joseph, 48, 49
Henschel, Virgil, 78, 125; Mrs.
  Virgil, 78
Hepner, John G., 74-76
Hibbard, George F., 76, 77; *see
  also* Carlson & Hibbard
Hickok (Hickox), David, 44, 45
High Prairie, 13
Highways, roads, stage lines, 25,
  44, 50, 55, 59-62, 65, 66, 70,
  74, 78, 83, 87-89, 92, 97, 104,
  108; Red Wing-Kenyon , 25,
  29, 31, 55; Red Wing-
  Zumbrota, , 50, 54, 60, 108; St.
  Paul & Dubuque, 71, 101; *see
  also* Railroads
Hill, James J., 90
Hillberg, Andrew C., 87
Hinkle, Charles, 46, 47
Hinz, Frederick H., 108
Hjermstad, H. M., 56; Hans, 13;
  Lars Sorenson, 117
Hoagland, George, 75
Hoff (Hauff), John, 47
Hogstad, Lyle, 13
Hoidahl, Joe, 57
Holden, x, 62-64, 89, 117; twp., 3,
  44, 69
Hole-in-the-Day, 30
Holmquist, O. S., 70
Holstad, Hans O., 56, 109; *see
  also* Rosvold & Holstad
Holst, Henry, 40
Holt, Edward, 57; Helen, 57
Horst, John (Rev.), 59
Hoverstad, Gertrude, 100
Hubbard, Lucius F., 52
Hubbard, Wells & Co., mill, 52
Huberty, cheese factory, 117; John
  B., 17
Hudson, Aaron G., 51
Hunt, A. J., 48; Cortland D., 15,
  47, 48; Earl, 48; S. A., 47
Huset, Nicholai O., 70; Ole D.,
  69; Ole H., 70
Hutcheson, David, 29
Hveem, Christian (Dr.), 11, 56
Hysell, Harry, 91

Independent Order of Good
  Templars (IOGT), 21
Irish settlers, 79

Jackson, Andrew P., 55
Jahn, Adam, 47, 48; Elizabeth, 48;
  Henry, 47, 48; Mrs. M., 47;
  Peter, 48
Jaishow, H. O., 56
Jameson, John W., 55
Jellum (Gjellum), Severt, 84
Jemtland, xi

Jenson, Anthon B., 23, 93
Jewitt, E. B., 46
Johnson, & Anderson, store, 103;
  Butler, 69; Carl O., 103;
  Charles, 87; Charles J., 93, 95;
  Frederick A., 38; Jesse A., 31;
  John, 94; John C., 93; Joseph,
  91; Lewis J., 103, 104; *see also*
  Benson & Johnson
Johnston, M. C., 51
Joint Powers Board, 22
Jones, A. T., 86
Julian, Clarence A., 96; store, *95*

Kellett, Thomas P., 7
Kelsey, & Charlton, creamery, 46;
  Byron, 46; J. H. & Bro., store,
  46; Joseph H., 46, 47; Lucinda
  (Brooks) (Mrs. Wilson), 46;
  Wilson, 46
Kenyon, viii, 4, 7, 26, 83, 90, 114;
  twp., 44, 80
Keyes, John, 32
Kinney, Colleen, 43; Georgene,
  43; Leo, 43; Val (Mrs. Leo),
  43; store, 43
Kleiber, Edward, 104, 125
Klossner, John, 68
Knights of Columbus Hall Asso-
  ciation, 17
Kolstad, J., 63; J. A., 100; Mary,
  100; Selma, 100
Kukacka, Vincent J., 91
Kulaas, P. T., 99-100; T. P., 100
Kunz, Dave, 27
Kvamme, Viola (Mrs. Dan), 104

Lajord, Thomas E., 63
Lake City, 38, 39, 72; creamery,
  24
Lake Pepin, 38, 72, 97
Lampert Yards, 19
Land O'Lakes, 19
Langness, Carl, 28; Signora (Mrs.
  Carl), 28
Larson, & Ohnstad, store, 56, 57;
  & Teigen, store, 57; John A.,
  93; Olaus, 56
Laverne, Frank, 109
Layng & Barsness, store, 15, 81
Leach, Herman, 110
Lee, A. A., 100; John, 71
Leet, Joseph T., 55
Lena (Lena Station), x, 64-66, 71,
  115, *65*; cheese factory, *64*;
  Dairy Association, 65
Lenzinger, A. O., 91; J. F., 91
Leon twp., 44, 101, 102
Lewis, C. M., 38; Silas S., 36
Leyh, George C., 90
Lien, Carl N., 100; Knute, 78
Lillesve, Lars, 86
Lime, 41

Lindberg, John, 107
Lindholm, Charles F., 21
Little Cannon River, 35, 36, 87
Live Stock Shippers Association, 91
Locke, Jabez Bradley, 67
Lockwood, Ephron, 31-33
Logan, Darryl, 59
Loomis, L. M., Co., 26, 27
Lostetter, Clara, 40; Harold, 40
Lowery, W. S., *41*, 42
Lund, I. O., 57
Lundberg family, 84
Lundeberg, K. O. (Rev.), 56

Maas, —, 117
Majerus, J. B., 17; Richard, 17; Wilfred, 17; businesses, 17, 19; Garage & Oil Co., 19
Manthei, William. 66
Mann, John, 44, 45
Mantorville, 4
Marko, Joseph, 100; Mildred, 100
Martenson, Esther, 107; family, 107; Ferdie, 107; Harry, 107; Nels, 107
Martin, Perry D., 38; Peter, 97
Marvin & Cammack, creamery, 47
Mason, J. R., 53; *see also* Rust & Mason
Mason, Olson & Engelhart, mill, 53
Matteson, C. C., 13
Mattson, Hans, 87
Mazeppa, 53, 65
McCadden, Alex, 81
McCardle, Richard, 22
McCorkell, William, 91
McCusker, Le Roy, 107
McGinnis, James, 7
McKenna, Leo, 107
McNamara, John V., 125
Melhuus (Melhouse), & Flesche, store, 99; Tosten A., 99
Merchant, A. A., 46
Merriam, Silas, 45, 46
Metz, Herman, 32, 33; John H., 33, 34; Joseph, 33; William, 33
Meyer, family, 59; George F., 59, 60; Machine Co., 59; mill, *60*; *see also* Hack & Meyer
Miami, x, xi, 66, 99
Miesville, 107
Miller, Gustaf O., 50, 106; John, 75; store, 106, 107, *105*; Telephone Co., 106
Miller & Lowery, mill, 42
Mills, Ida, 42; Lydia (Mrs. Warren), 42; Warren, 41, 42
Milwaukee Elevator Co., 26, 27
Mineral Springs, xi
Minneapolis, 72

Minneola, 66-68; twp., x, 26, 44, 66, 67
Minnesota Highway Department, 115
Minnesota Malting Co., 40, 109, 110
Minnesota State Railroad & Warehouse Commission, 110
Minnesota Stoneware co., 39
Mississippi River, 30, 52
Mix, Clara G., 29
Modern Woodmen of America, 83, 106
Moe, Bennie, 57; Charles N., 38
Mohr & Sons, motorcycles, 59
Monson, Andrew, 83; Mons F., 105, 106
Moran, Thomas, 108
Morell, Alfred, 46
Morgan, Thomas, 65
Mossville, 4, 117
Muhlman, Claus, 60
Murphy, Effie M., 53
Mutz, — (Mr.), 54
Myhre, Knut M., 100; Knut N., 33

Nansen, Fridtjof, 68
Nansen, x, 68, 69, 115; cheese factory, 68, *69*; Cooperative Dairy Association, 69
National Matrimonial Agency, 48
Nelson, Earl, 125; Elaine, 92; Evelyn (Wendler) (Mrs. Ray H.), 124; Harris, 104; Henry W., 91, 92; hotel, 90; Lucelle, 104; Samuel, 8; Solomon, 94; store, 92; Virgil W., 91
Nerison, Pauline, 125
Nerstrand, 90
Nesheim, Nils L., 100
Nesseth, Clarence, 100; Helen, 100
Nesson (Nessen), Jacob N. 14, 76; Laurits, 40
New Bellechester, 17
New Jerusalem, 64
Nichols, Charles H., 62; George M., 62, 63
Nilan, Edward P., 43; Helen M., 43; Martin G., 43; Michael T., 42; Michael T., Jr., 43; store, 42, *43*
Norby, B. O., 13; N., 12; Walt, 57
Nordvold, Olaf O., 108
Norelius, John, 93, 95
North Star Stoneware, 39
Northfield, 89
Norway, 44, 69, 70, *71*
Norwegian settlers, 44, 69, 93, 99, 116, 117
Nygaard, Chris, 57; Oscar, 104

Oak Center, 19

Oelkers, Joe, 60
Ofelt, Nathan B., 95; store, 95, *94*, *95*
Ohnstad (Onstad), John, 68; Joseph O., 56; Ole, 69; *see also* Larson & Ohnstad
Old Country Store, 92
Oleson, O. C., 24
Olson, Andrew, 67; Glenn, 125; Hans P., 55; Nels M., 52; P., 106; *see also* Brusegaard & Olson; Mason, Olson & Engelhart
Opsal, Martin T., *see* Thompson, Martin
Orange Jug, store, 98
Oronoco, 4, 30, 54
Orr, B. E., 33, 34; David H., 32-35; Ervin G., 33
Orr, D. H., & Son, 33
Otterness, John H., 26, 27, 86; *see also* Charlson Brothers & Otterness
Overby, — (Mr.), 83
Owatonna, 4
Oxford Mills, x, 14, 32, 34-37; mill ruins, *37*

Palmer, H. H., 51
Panic of 1857, 31, 74; of 1893, 73
Parker, Charles, 92; James W., 30; Truman, 71, 92
Parkin, Arthur W., 66; Edgar A., 66
Paul, John, 39
Paulson, James, 57; John, 87, 93
Pearson, Nels, 78
Pease, Elam, 66
Petersdorf, A. W., 21
Peterson, Gustefnus, 87; Olaf J., 68; Otto, 77; Per A., 107; Peter, 108; Reinholdt, 42
Petterson, Sven P., 87
Phillips, Robert L., 38
Pierce, Joshua C., 55
Pine Island, 7; twp., 64, 71, 117
Poncelet, Adam, 19, 20; David, 17; Joseph, 16
Poplar Grove, 30, 71, 72, 117; church, 72, *71*; Dairy Association, 72
Post, Abner W., 97; George, 97; May R. S., 97
Potter, Calvin, 50
Prairie Creek, 89
Prairie Island, 42-44
Pratt, James, 71
Prigge, Albert, 125
Purdy, Dorothy, 78; George, 78; William H., 56
Pye, Harlan, 91; R. W., 91; W. W., 91
Pynten, L. H., 68; Ole H., 68

Quimby, Orville, 124

Railroads, 25, 26, 62, 64, 65, 97, 107, 108, 110, 111; Chicago & North Western, 65; Chicago Great Western (CGW), 17, 65, 83, 84, 90, 91, 117; Chicago, Milwaukee & St. Paul, 32, 42, 44, 67, 88, 106; Chicago, Milwaukee, St. Paul & Pacific, 8, 25; Duluth, Red Wing & Southern, 8, 39, 54, 60, 65, 108; Great Northern, 90; Minnesota & Northwestern, 8, 34, 90; Minnesota Central, 21, 22, 32, 90; Minnesota Midland, 25, 52; Rochester & Northern Minnesota, 64, 65; St. Paul & Dubuque, 3, 30, 71, 117; St. Paul Southern Electric, 86, 107; *see also* Highways, roads, stage lines
Ramsey, Alexander, 30
Randolph, 34, 90; opera house, 34
Rathkey, Charles, 46
Red Wing, 3, 4, 7, 8, 20, 25, 29, 31, 44, 45, 52, 96-98, 109
Red Wing-Kenyon stage line, *see* Highways
Red Wing Malting Co., 17
Red Wing Pottery, 39, 68
Red Wing Sewer Pipe Co., 17, 39
Red Wing Stoneware Co., 39
Red Wing Union Stoneware Co., 39
Red Wing-Zumbrota road, *see* Highways
Rest Island, 72, 73
Rest Islander, The, periodical, 72, 73
Rice, Constant, 78; Silas W., 78; W. C. (Rev.), 108; William J., 21
Rice, 108
Rice Lake, 4
Richards, G. I., 98
Richardson, Bob, 78; Judy (Purdy; Mrs. Bob), 78
Roads, *see* Highways
Roberts, Asahel D., 50
Roch, John, 87
Rochester, 20, 65
Rockne, A. J. (Sen.), 104
Roe, Charles O., 28
Rogers, Alfred, 75
Rogne, Knute T., 63
Roland, Nils, 12
Romness, Brothers, store, 77; Halvor, 77; Nelson (Nels) O., 77
Ronningen, W. W., 70
Root, Byington, 88; Duane S., 88
Rosby, J. & Bros., store, 42

Roscoe, ix, x, 4, 15, 74-78, 92, 101, 115; Butter & Cheese Factory, 77; Dairy Association, 78; literary/debating society, 76; Mounted Militia, 75; store, 77; twp., 44, 74, 75, 78, 93
Roscoe Center/Centre, x, 78, 79, 92, 114, 115; Butter & Cheese Association, 78, factory, 79; Stordahl Lutheran Church, 78
Rosing, & Doyle, store, 25; Orvar G., 25; *see also* Sandberg & Rosing
Rosvold, Andrew, 56
Rosvold & Holstad, store, 56
Rural free delivery (RFD), 4, 5, 13, 24, 57, 62, 63, 68, 86, 95, 98, 109, 113
Ruskin, 26, 27
Russell, — (Miss), 48; E. A. (Mrs.), 72, 73; Elisha, 46; Ida (Mrs. J. F.), 47; U. V., 46; see also Eastman & Russell
Rust, John R., 52
Rust & Mason, mill, 52
Rust Milling Co., mill, 52
Ruud, Arnold, 28; Mabel, 28; Martin J., 28
Ryan, Catherine, *80*; Elizabeth, *80*; Jim, *80*; Philip, 25, 79, 80, *80*; Sarah, *80*
Ryan, 79, 80, 115; post office, *80*; St. Columbkill's Catholic Church, 79
Ryden (Rydin), Gustaf/Gustaff A., 56, 103

St. Columbkill's Catholic Church, *see* Ryan
St. Paul, 107
Sandberg, & Rosing, store, 103; John H. (Dr.), 94
Sands, Henry, 12
Santleman, Henry, 40; William, 40; store, 22, 40
Sargent, Edwin A., 101
Saunders, Daniel, 97
Saupe, Edward, 98
Saville, Dora, 98; Edward, 98
Sawyer, Willis R., 18
Schafer, Agnes (Miss), 110
Scharpen, Duane, 57; Mary, 57
Scherf, Ernestine, 98; Fred A., 98; store, 98
Scherz & Heigle, cheese factory, 27
Schneebeli, Casper, 75
Schools, 29, 30, 34, 38, 44, 53, 60, 64, 75, 86, 89, 91, 96, 98, 104, 114, *29, 49*
Schultz, Joseph, 59
Schwieger, Thomas, 21

Scofield, Arlin A., 33; Grace (Mrs.), 125; M. G., 46
Scott, Joseph, 38
Sevareid, Erick Erickson, 117
Sevastopol, x, 98
Sevill, Willard, 38
Shades of Sherwood, camp-ground, 68
Sheets, Albert E., 99, 100; George E., 99, 100
Shepard, Frank, 28; William, 28
Sherwood, Charles A., 47, 49
Sibley, Henry Hastings, 30
Simpson, David, 14; Ellen M. (Mrs.), 15; James, 15
Skillestad, Claremont, 28; Esther, 28
Skyberg, Simon O., 80, 81
Skyberg, viii-x, 15, 28, 80-84, 91, 107, 115; Cooperative Creamery Association, 81, 83, *83*; Meyer store, 83
Smith, Arthur, 124; Daniel C., 14; James B., 97; Otis F., 55; William P., 78
Sogn, ix, x, 26, 84-87, 100, 101, 115, 116; Cooperative Dairy Association, 85; store, *85, 86*
Sones, Ellen M. (Mrs.), 53
Spencer, 87-89, 93
Spinney, Joseph D., 50
Spring Creek, x, 15, 27, 88, 89, 109
Spreiter, Mrs. Arthur, 125
Spring Garden, xi
Stage lines, *see* Highways
Stanton, Edward, 38; George, 38; John, 89; William, 89
Stanton, ix, x, 89-92, 107, 115, 117; Creamery & Cheese Factory, 90; Flats, 89; Methodist Church, 92; State Bank, 91; twp, 31, 89, 90
Stecher, Theodore, 53
Steffa, Reuben J., 80
Stene, John J., 63
Stene & Glemme, store, 63
Stenhaug, Adolph, 87, 125; T., 100; Ted, 86
Stephenson, Robert, 81
Sterling, V. W., 46
Sterritt, Frank, 38
Stickney, Alpheus Beede, 90
Stockwell, B., 46
Stone, Ellery, 101; F. S., 104; Israel, 101; S. E., 104
Storseth, Thomas P., 56
Strand, & Skreen, store, 100; Christopher T., 100
Strandness, Jacob O., 88
Strauss, Clem, 17, 19; Frank M., 17, 18; Matt, 17; Nick, 17, 19; businesses, 17-19

Strom, blacksmith shop, 107; F.
A., 91; Gilbert S., 106
Stroms, xi
Stussy, Jacob, 47
Sunapee, 78, 92, 93
Sundry, Tollef O., 77
Sutherland, James, 50; Solomon,
14
Swanson, & Roe, lumberyard, 18;
C. E., 107; Charles B., 83;
Ernest L., 86
Swarts, Arthur H., 91; Robert J.,
91
Sweatland, E., 55
Swedish settlement, 96
Swinton, Amos W., 91
Syverson, Berdela (Mrs. Ken-
neth), 125

Taft, A. W., 46
Talla, Henry Nelson, 117
Tappen, Arthur, 67
Teigen, Ole T., 57; *see also*
Larson & Teigen
Terrell, Henry K., 101, 105, 117
Thomas, John, 89
Thomforde, Fred, 24
Thompson, C., 56; Etta, 72, 73;
Martin (T. Opsal), 101-104;
Thomas B., 68, 69; Thomas E.,
62, 63
Thoten, 23, 93
Thurber, Etta M., 97
Tiller, Conrad, 57; Joseph R., 57
Tillman, Christ, 60
Timolat, Harry N., 72
Tolstad, Louis A., 91
Townsend, P. B., 76
Troombly (Twombley, Twombly),
Albra, 66
Trout Brook, xi
Troy, x, 30, 31, 45
Troy, Winona Co., 117
Troy City, 30
Tvedt, Even J., 99
Tveitmoe, Ola A., 84
Twin Cities Milk Producers Asso-
ciation, 91
Twombly, Louisa (Mrs.), 67

Underdahl, Hans, 68; John O., 84;
L. H., 125
Uslar, George, 54

Van Dusen Elevator Co., 64
Vandenburgh, Philander, 30
Vanderwalker, Ancil (Ansel), 47-
49
Vang, church, 63
Vasa, ix, x, 87, 93-95, 115, 116;
Farmers' Union, 87, 93, 105;
House/Hotel, 93; store, *94*;
twp., xi, 22, 87, 93, 105

Vermillion Creamery Co., 43
Vinton, Samuel B., 89
Voxland, Helmer, 27

Wa-coo-ta, 7, 97
Wabasha, 25, 52
Wabasha County, 15, 16, 20
Wacouta (Wacoota), ix, 96-98,
115; twp., 97, 98
Wait, Beriah C., 88; Walter B., 88
Walbridge, V. M., 34
Wales, Shubael, 55
Wanamingo, 8, 25-27; twp., 3, 11,
26, 44, 55, 69, 70, 88, 117;
twp. hall, 13, *10*
Wangen, Carl J., 13, 124; cheese
factory, 13; John T., 13
Wangen Prairie Lutheran Church,
see Aurland
Wangs, ix, x, 33, 66, 84, 89, 99-
101, 115, 117; store, *99*
Warsaw twp., 13, 31, 44, 66, 84,
99
Wasioja, 4
Wastedo, ix, x, 74, 90, 96, 101-
105, 114, 115, 117; Creamery
Co., 104; store, *102, 103*
Webb, Martin L., 75; Oliver, 74
Webster Cooperative Dairy Asso-
ciation, 22, 87
Wedge Lumber Co., 19
Welch, x, 8, 22, 41-43, 91, 96,
107; twp., 8, 42
Welch Station, xi
Wells, William S., 51, 52; *see also*
Hubbard, Wells & Co.
Wells Creek, 23
Wells Creek Mills, xi
West Concord, 82
West Red Wing, xi
Westby, Marcus J., 31
Wester, Julius, 106
Westermo, Hans C., *see*
Christensen, Hans
Western, G., 100
Westerson (Westerton), John, 106;
William H., 106
Westervelt, Evert, 7
Westervelt, 3, 7
White, Francis J., 81-83
White Rock, ix, x, 22, 93, 105-
107, 109, 115, 116; Creamery
Association, 106; Farmers'
Commercial Union, 105;
Miller store, *105*; State Bank,
19, 91, 106, 107
White Willow, x, 50, 108-111,
115; Dairy Association cheese
factory, 111, *110*; house, *109*
Whitson, John A., 31; William, 32
Whitson & Byrnes, mill, 31
Wickum, R. H., 27
Widmey, John E., 63

Wilcox, Charles N., 35-37; *see
also* Archibald & Wilcox
Wilks, — (Mr.), 108
Willard, Frances E., 72
Willard Cottage, *see* Rest Island
Williams, Alvin D., 45, 46; John,
47
Williamson, William A., 11
Wing, Osmund J., 11, 27
Winston, E. J. (Dr.), 14
Winter, Richard, 111
Wisconsin Cheese Producers
Federation, 66
Wolpers, Henry, 59
Woodbury, Ed, 109
Woolley, John G., 72, 73
Works Progress Administration
(WPA), 68
World War I, 28
World War II, 24, 94, 107
Wunderlich, John, 47; Martin, 47
Wyman, J. K., 46

Yngsdal, Elmer, 28; Ole, 28
Young, Milton, 51
York twp., 45

Zeller, Kenneth, 49, 57
Zemke, Charles J., 109, 111;
Herman, 109; store, 110
Zumbro River, 51, 52, 68, 89
Zumbrota, 4, 7, 8, 24, 25, 28, 35,
44, 45, 52, 55, 57, 65, 88, 92,
107, 114; Brick & Tile Co., 67;
Clay Manufacturing Co., 67;
Hammer creamery, 24; twp.,
66, 108; *see also* Highways,
roads, stage lines; Railroads

About the Author

Roy W. Meyer grew up in Goodhue County, attended a rural school, and graduated from Zumbrota High School before serving in the U.S. Army in World War II. He earned a bachelor's degree at St. Olaf College in Northfield, Minnesota, and a master's degree and a doctorate at the University of Iowa. He taught at State Teachers College, Valley City, North Dakota, and at Minnesota State University, Mankato, and held a Fulbright appointment at Flinders University of South Australia. He received the Minnesota Historical Society's Solon J. Buck Prize twice and the Western History Association Award once for *Minnesota History* articles published in 1961, 1968, and 1974.

Also by Roy W. Meyer

The Middle Western Farm Novel in the Twentieth Century

History of the Santee Sioux: United States Indian Policy on Trial

The Village Indians of the Upper Missouri: The Mandans, Hidatsas, and Arikaras

Everyone's Country Estate: A History of Minnesota's State Parks